Great Men
of God

(From Elijah to the Fall of Jerusalem)

VOLUME FIVE

the Bible Story

Great Men of God ❖ Volume Five

Arthur S. Maxwell
Author of Uncle Arthur's *Bedtime Stories*

When Arthur S. Maxwell wrote *The Bible Story*, he used the King James Version of the Bible, closely following its narrative. This edition continues that tradition and draws from other translations using language that today's children readily understand.

NEWLY REVISED AND ILLUSTRATED

More than 400 stories in 10 Volumes Covering the Entire Bible From Genesis to Revelation

REVIEW AND HERALD® PUBLISHING ASSOCIATION
HAGERSTOWN, MD 21740

Illustrations not individually
credited are by Fred Collins,
Kreigh Collins, Klem Gretter,
Russell Harlan, Iris Johnson,
Manning de V. Lee, Paul
Remmey, and Herbert Rudeen.

Unless otherwise noted, all
Bible verses are from the *Holy
Bible, New International Version*.
Copyright © 1973, 1978, 1983,
International Bible Society.
Used by permission of
Zondervan Bible Publishers.
Bible texts credited to TEV are
from the *Good News Bible*—
Old Testament: Copyright ©
American Bible Society 1976;
New Testament: Copyright ©
American Bible Society 1966,
1971, 1976.

This book was
Revised by Cheryl Holloway
Edited by Eugene Lincoln
Cover art by Harry Anderson

PRINTED IN U.S.A.

R&H Cataloging Service
Maxwell, Arthur Stanley,
1896-1970
    The Bible story.
    1. Bible stories.   I. Title.
II. Holloway, Cheryl Woolsey,
1956-
        220.9505

ISBN 0-8280-0799-3

Under wise teachers in the synagogue schools boys and girls of the
Jewish nation received moral instruction and training in useful arts
that would make them leaders of their people.

PAINTING BY RUSSELL HARLAN

C O N T E N T S

PART ONE—Stories of Elijah

PART TWO—Stories of Elisha

PART THREE—Stories of Conflict and Blessing

PART FOUR—Stories of Kings and Prophets

PART ONE

Stories of

Elijah

(1 Kings 17:1-2 Kings 2:15)

Boy With a Wonderful Name

(1 Kings 17:1)

NOT LONG after King Solomon died, a little boy was born in the land of Gilead, east of the Jordan River. The Bible does not tell us anything about his parents, not even their names. But they must have been very good people, because they called their precious little son Elijah, which means "My God is the Lord." No doubt his parents dedicated him to God from his birth and prayed that he would grow up to be a brave and noble champion of truth and right.

From time to time in their little home far from Jerusalem, they heard about the dreadful things going on in the holy city. The idol worship that Solomon's wives had introduced had spread all over Israel and Judah. But Elijah's parents made up their minds that whatever happened, they would remain true to the Lord, the God of Abraham, Isaac, Jacob—and David.

While Elijah was growing up, people were taking sides between the God of heaven and the gods of the heathen.

9

← PAINTING BY RUSSELL HARLAN

In the midst of the idolatry and wickedness of Israel the parents of Elijah taught him to worship the true God, and God called him to be one of the great prophets to His people.

There were even reports that Jeroboam, the new king of Israel, had made golden calves and told the people that these were the gods that brought them out of Egypt.

As Elijah talked with other boys he knew, some of them would say, "We worship Baal; he's the best god." Others said, "We like Ashtoreth better; you should just see what goes on in front of that idol." And still others, "We go to Molech's temple; things are much more exciting there." Then Elijah would say very bravely, "But my God is the Lord."

The more he saw of the evil things the people did as they worshiped their idols, the more sure he was that he was right. How could the people be so blind, so stupid, he wondered, as to think that God was pleased with all this wickedness? How could they believe that He wanted little children burned as sacrifices in the temple of Molech? It was all so wrong, so very wrong, that it made Elijah decide to give himself, his life, everything he had, to teaching the people about the true God.

As he talked with other boys and girls, mixed with the people in village market places, or sat alone on the mountainside, he would tell himself again and again, "My God is the Lord, my God is the Lord."

His name became part of himself. And people came to know him as the strange lad who hated idols and worshiped the God of heaven. They said he was old-fashioned and out-of-date. They told him he wouldn't get anywhere in life if he held onto such foolish ideas. But God's eye was on him. Here was a boy He could use. Here was the champion He was looking for!

And what a destiny was his!

Today, nearly 3,000 years later, the eyes of the Lord still "range throughout the earth to strengthen those whose hearts are fully committed to him." * He is still listening eagerly for those precious words of loyalty "My God is the Lord!" Blessed are the boys and girls who speak them from love-filled hearts. What a destiny lies before *them!* How much God will do for them, here and hereafter!

You too can be a boy—or a girl—with a wonderful name. Just make the same decision Elijah did. Say, "My God is the Lord"—and mean it.

---

* 2 Chronicles 16:9.

God's Messenger

(*1 Kings 17:1; 18:10*)

FAR FROM the cities of Judah and Israel, out in the rugged, unsettled region of Gilead, Elijah grew to manhood. Like John the Baptist, who lived in the same place years afterward, he didn't have many of life's comforts. Food was scarce. Clothes were hard to get. His only luxury was talking with God.

Many times he must have wondered why God did not do something about all the wickedness in the country. Many times he must have looked up into the skies and cried, "How long, O Lord, how long?"

At last God spoke—as He always does when His time has come. He told Elijah to go to Ahab, now king of Israel, and tell him that because of his sins a great drought would come upon the country. There would be neither dew nor rain for years.

It was not a pleasant message to take to a king, but Elijah fearlessly set out to deliver it. Without a thought of danger to himself, he made his way over the mountain trails to Samaria, where Ahab had set up his new capital and built a temple to Baal.

Arriving in the city, he walked up the busy main street that led to the palace on the hill. Passing the guards at the gate, he entered the hall where the king was sitting on his throne, with many courtiers around him.

Quickly all eyes turned to the stranger who had suddenly appeared before them. Who was this man dressed in a rough garment of hair and a leather belt? What was he doing in the king's court?

Everyone soon found out. The prophet's message was short. In a loud, powerful voice, Elijah declared, "As the Lord, the God of Israel, lives, whom I serve, there will be neither dew nor rain in the next few years except at my word."

What happened next we are not told. But there must have been quite a stir.

"Is the man mad?" Ahab may well have said. "Does he think he can control the dew and the rain? Does he think his God is stronger than Baal?" At this the courtiers laughed, jeering at Elijah as he made his way to the door and disappeared.

But Elijah's warning was no laughing matter. The dry weather began, just as he said it would. Day after day the sun beat down upon the parched land out of a cloudless sky.

There was no dew at night or rain during the day. Soon the whole countryside looked brown and dry.

Not a single green blade of grass managed to survive. Cattle roamed far and wide looking for something to eat. Streams ran dry. The water level in wells dropped alarmingly as autumn failed to bring the rainy season. The land was almost too hard to plow. Farmers sowed seed they had saved from the grain crop of the year before, but it hardly began to grow before it shriveled up.

Winter came and passed, and still there was no rain. People watched the clouds hopefully, but they passed over and left no moisture. The usual spring harvest failed to appear.

Cattle began to die by the hundreds. The bodies of bony cows, sheep, and goats lay unburied for the crows and vultures to eat.

Everybody, from the king in his palace to the humblest shepherd on the hills, was worried. All of them knew that they were facing starvation and ruin. But instead of praying to God, they turned to Baal, Ashtoreth, and Molech. "Send us rain!" they cried to their idols, but no rain came.

Another blazing summer passed, another scorching autumn, another winter of rainless clouds passing overhead. Would there never be an end to this dreadful drought? people

wondered. Must Palestine turn into a desert?

Many times King Ahab thought about the man who had come to see him in his palace—the man who had claimed to be a prophet of the Lord and had said there would be no dew or rain unless he said so. Perhaps he *did* know how to control the weather. Perhaps he was able to keep rain from falling on the earth. Where was he? He had to be found. He must be made to break the spell he had put on the country.

So Ahab set a price on Elijah's head and sent out orders for the prophet to be brought to Samaria at once. But nobody could find him. He had disappeared. Growing more and more desperate, the king sent messengers to Egypt, to Aram, to Mesopotamia, to hunt for Elijah. There wasn't "a nation or kingdom" where Ahab's messengers did not go to search for him.

As the messengers returned they all told the same story. They had failed in their mission. There was no trace of Elijah anywhere. Nobody had seen him or heard of him.

"Where can the man be?" fumed Ahab. "He must be somewhere. Find him!"

But no one could. Yet he wasn't far away. And God knew where he was all the time. ✑

Fed by Ravens

(1 Kings 17:2-9)

WHEN Elijah left Ahab's palace, God said to him, "Leave here, turn eastward and hide in the Kerith Ravine, east of the Jordan. You will drink from the brook, and I have ordered the ravens to feed you there."

Elijah knew the Kerith Ravine very well. He had probably played on its banks as a boy. He remembered the ravens too and where they nested.

It was a long, tiring journey back across the Jordan, but eventually Elijah found the wild canyon God had described in the mountains beyond the river. He followed the tiny stream that ran along the bottom of the ravine until he came to a cave or an overhanging rock, where he stopped to rest. He was certain that Ahab could never find him here.

It was a lonesome, desolate spot, and quiet, except for the distant cawing of the ravens and the tinkling of the stream as it cascaded over rocks and pebbles toward the Jordan. There was no trace of man or woman, boy or girl. He was alone, utterly alone, with God.

16

Growing hungry, he wondered where he
could find something to eat. But there wasn't
any food, and he didn't dare betray his hiding place by going to
search for some. The hours slipped by. Evening came. Just
when it seemed as though he had to go to sleep without a bite to
eat, a raven flew overhead and dropped something. Elijah
picked it up. It was food. How thankful he was!

It was strange that a raven would act like this! Perhaps it
was just an accident. But no—it could not be, for here came
another, and another, each dropping some delicious piece of
bread or meat that normally it would have eaten.

Elijah looked up and saw the food falling out of the sky as if it were falling from heaven. Then he remembered God's promise to command the ravens to feed him. His heart overflowed with thankfulness. "My God is the Lord," he may well have said. "Wonderful, wonderful God!"

In the morning the same thing happened. As the sun rose above the canyon walls the ravens came flying in low again, dropping their little offerings of food to this man who was a friend of God.

"The ravens brought him bread and meat in the morning and bread and meat in the evening, and he drank from the brook." Day after day this wonderful thing happened, and Elijah marveled more and more at the goodness of God in looking after him so faithfully.

Much of the time he spent down by the brook, where the cool water helped him bear the terrible heat. As time passed and no rain fell, the stream gradually got smaller and smaller, more and more shallow. Some nights he could scarcely hear its gurgle anymore.

He knew then that he would soon have to leave this hiding place and find another. But where could he go? Where would he be safe from the anger of Ahab? He did not need to worry. God was thinking of him and planning for him.

Finally, when the last little trickle of water had disappeared and the last little pool in the bed of the brook had dried up, God said to him, "Go at once to Zarephath

of Sidon and stay there. I have commanded a widow in that place to supply you with food."

Elijah understood. God was sending him far north of Samaria to a little city near the coast. Saying goodbye to his raven friends and gathering up their last little gifts of love—for he knew he would find no food on his journey—he set out for Zarephath.

Day after day he trudged on over rocky hillsides and steep mountain trails. How tired he must have been! How hungry! How very, very thirsty!

Weary, hot, and dusty, he came at last to Zarephath. Now he could see the outline of the city wall; now the gate he would have to enter. How glad he was that his long journey was almost over! But how would he find the woman who was to care for him?

God had not told him her name or where she lived. Was she rich or poor, old or young? All he knew about her was that she was a widow—and there must be many widows in Zarephath. How would he know the right one? With Ahab's soldiers looking for him everywhere, he must not make a mistake.

The Never-Empty Jar

(1 Kings 17:10-24)

AS ELIJAH was wondering what to do next he saw a woman gathering sticks not far from the city gate. He called to her and asked, "Would you bring me a little water in a jar so I may have a drink?"

Looking up, the woman saw the dusty stranger. Feeling sorry for him, she hurried off to get some water. As she did she heard him calling to her again.

"Bring me something to eat, too," he said.

The woman stopped and slowly turned to face him. "As surely as the Lord your God lives," she said sadly, "I don't have any bread—only a handful of flour in a jar and a little oil in a jug. I am gathering a few sticks to take home and make a meal for myself and my son, that we may eat it—and die."

Elijah could see she was telling him the truth, and he was sorry for her. He felt sure now that this must be the widow God had asked to feed him. And she was so poor she had nothing in the world except a handful of flour and a little oil! Elijah knew something wonderful was sure to happen soon.

21

◄— PAINTING BY RUSSELL HARLAN

During the time of terrible famine in Israel a poor widow shared her last loaf of bread with the prophet Elijah and God honored her faith by keeping her jars full of oil and meal.

"Don't be afraid," he said kindly to the poor widow. "Go home and do as you have said. But first make a small cake of bread for me from what you have and bring it to me, and then make something for yourself and your son. For this is what the Lord, the God of Israel, says: 'The jar of flour will not be used up and the jug of oil will not run dry until the day the Lord gives rain on the land.' "

It may have sounded selfish for him to say, "First make a small cake of bread for me," but it really wasn't. Elijah's faith in God was so great that to him the jar of flour was already full and the jug of oil was overflowing. He was absolutely sure that if the poor widow trusted God's promise enough to make him a little bread *first*, then God would continue to bless her in many wonderful ways.

The widow decided to trust God. She took Him at His word. Going to her house, she looked into the flour jar. Just as she had told Elijah, there was only a handful left at the bottom of it. She scraped it out into a little pile. Then she went to the oil jug. Tipping it up, she drained out the last drop, or so she thought.

After mixing the oil and flour into a paste, she prepared to light the fire. Perhaps her son came running in just then. I can hear him saying, "Is that bread for me, Mamma?"

"No, darling, it's for the man of God who has come to see us."

"But I'm hungry."

"I know, dear, but he has promised me that God won't let us starve."

The fire blazed up, and the woman put the dough on the hot bricks. It began to brown, and soon filled the little kitchen with a sweet aroma.

Suddenly there was an excited cry from the boy. "Mamma, I thought you said there was no more flour in the jar, but there is!"

"No, darling, there can't be. I scraped the last of it out just now."

"But there is, there is! See, Mamma! It's nice, new flour, too!"

The poor widow looked in the jar and could hardly believe her eyes. There *was* flour there! More than there had been for many days. She turned to the jug of oil and tipped it up. Oil flowed out. It was too wonderful! Joy filled her heart.

She looked over at Elijah, sitting there waiting for his meal. There was a beautiful smile on his tired face, a smile of sheer delight that God had honored his faith so soon. Not only

Elijah ate that night, but so did the widow and her son. They had not enjoyed such a good meal in many days.

And because the widow did as Elijah had told her, "there was food every day for Elijah and for the woman and her family. For the jar of flour was not used up and the jug of oil did not run dry, in keeping with the word of the Lord spoken by Elijah."

What a wonderful time the angels must have had putting flour in that jar and filling up that jug of oil! How happy they must have been watching the surprise on the widow's face when she discovered what had happened!

But this was not the only blessing God sent because of her kindness to His servant.

One day her son became very ill. Lovingly she tended him, but he became worse and worse. Feeling sure he was dying, she took him in her arms, and there he breathed his last breath.

"Elijah! Elijah!" she cried. The man of God came down from the loft where he was living. He saw at once what had happened.

"Give me your son," he said to the widow, taking the limp body from the sobbing mother.

He climbed up into the loft again and laid the boy on his bed. "Then he stretched himself out on the boy three times and cried to the Lord, 'O Lord my God, let this boy's life return to him!'

"The Lord heard Elijah's cry, and the boy's life returned to him, and he lived. Elijah picked up the child and carried

him down from the room into the house."

Speechless with grief, the poor widow scarcely noticed Elijah as he climbed down from the loft again with the boy in his arms.

Then she heard the prophet speak to her. What was it he was saying?

"Look, your son is alive!"

"What? Impossible!" She rushed across the room.

It was true, true! He was alive! He was breathing again! Oh, joy! Tears of happiness and gratitude streamed down her cheeks as she cried, "Now I know that you are a man of God and that the word of the Lord from your mouth is the truth."

Fire From Heaven

(1 Kings 18:1-39)

THREE years had passed since Elijah had stood in King Ahab's court and announced the coming of the great drought. Part of this time he had spent by the Kerith Ravine, and the rest he had spent with the widow of Zarephath.

Many times during these lonely days he must have wondered what God was planning to do next for His people. Had they learned their lesson yet? Were they ready to turn from their idols? Someday the drought must end, but how and when?

At last the word of the Lord came to him, saying, "Go and present yourself to Ahab, and I will send rain on the land."

Elijah set out at once for Samaria, 150 miles or so to the south of Zarephath. On the way he ran into Obadiah, the man in charge of Ahab's palace. He was searching for pasture for the horses and mules that were still alive.

This good man was one of the few leaders who remained

26

loyal to the God of heaven. He had shown his loyalty by hiding 100 of God's prophets in a cave when Queen Jezebel had tried to kill them. Recognizing Elijah, he dropped to his knees and cried, "Is it really you, my lord Elijah?"

"Yes," replied Elijah. "Go tell your master, 'Elijah is here.'"

"I can't," said Obadiah. He was afraid. Ahab, he said, had been searching everywhere for Elijah. There had been many false reports as to where he had been seen, and these had just made the king more and more angry. "If I tell Ahab you are here," Obadiah said, "and he finds you have disappeared again, he will kill me."

"As the Lord Almighty lives, whom I serve," said Elijah, "I will surely present myself to Ahab today."

Obadiah believed him and rode off to find the king. When he heard the news, Ahab hurried to the place where his servant had said he would find Elijah. The prophet was still there.

"Is that you, you troubler of Israel?" he demanded angrily as he drew up his horse close to Elijah.

"I have not made trouble for Israel," replied Elijah without flinching. "But you and your father's family have. You have abandoned the Lord's commands and have followed the Baals." Elijah explained to Ahab what he must do if he wanted to know the blessing of God again.

"Now summon the people from all over Israel to meet me on Mount Carmel. And bring the four hundred and fifty prophets of Baal and the four hundred prophets of Asherah, who eat at Jezebel's table."

The king agreed to the plan. Perhaps he thought that it was his only hope of getting rain and breaking the dreadful drought. When he returned to his palace, he sent out messengers calling the people to assemble at Mount Carmel.

Soon thousands of men, women, and children were streaming toward the place of meeting. No one was quite sure why they were going there, except that the king had told them to. There was a rumor that Elijah would be there, but nobody believed it. Similar tales had been told about the prophet for the past three years, and he had never shown up. Hadn't the king himself been looking for him all this time?

Pushing and jostling one another, the people climbed up toward the top of Mount Carmel until all the slopes were covered. All night long they stayed there, waiting for the dawn.

28

Early in the morning somebody cried, "There he is! I can see him! Elijah is here!"

Instantly the word swept through the waiting throng. Men and women strained their necks to see the man who had dared to defy the king, while boys and girls shoved their way to the front to get a better view.

"Hush!" cried someone. "Hush! He's speaking. Elijah is speaking."

Silence fell over the milling crowd. Then from the top of the mountain came that powerful voice once heard in Ahab's court.

"How long will you waver between two opinions?" cried the prophet. "If the Lord is God, follow him; but if Baal is God, follow him."

Nobody spoke.

Elijah continued, "I am the only one of the Lord's prophets left, but Baal has four hundred and fifty prophets. Get two bulls for us. Let them choose one for themselves, and let them cut it into pieces and put it on the wood but not set fire to it. I will prepare the other bull and put it on the wood but not set fire to it. Then you call on the name of your god, and

I will call on the name of the Lord. The god who answers by fire—he is God."

"Well said; that's fair enough," cried the people, thrilled to learn that they were to see such a test of the powers of rival gods. From now on they watched and listened with 10 times as much interest.

Turning to the prophets of Baal, Elijah said to them, "Choose one of the bulls and prepare it first, since there are so many of you. Call on the name of your god, but do not light the fire."

Glad for the chance to prove that Baal was the greatest god on earth, his prophets seized their bull, cut it up, and placed the pieces on the altar they had built.

Then they began to implore their god to send fire to burn the sacrifice. "O Baal, answer us!" they shouted.

"But there was no response; no one answered."

They started to leap up and down around the altar, crying, "O Baal, answer us!" but still no fire came.

All morning long they kept up the wild dancing and shouting. "At noon Elijah began to taunt them. 'Shout

louder!' he said. 'Surely he is a god! Perhaps he is deep in thought, or busy, or traveling. Maybe he is sleeping and must be awakened.' "

At this they cried still louder and began to cut themselves with knives "until their blood flowed." It did no good. Midday passed. Afternoon came. The sun began to sink toward the gray-green sea. Still "there was no response, no one answered, no one paid attention."

At last Elijah spoke again to the people, who were tired and disappointed in the failure of the prophets of Baal. "Come here to me," he cried, and the crowd surged forward.

They watched him repair the altar of the Lord that had been standing on Mount Carmel for many years but had been forgotten. Taking 12 stones, one for each of the 12 tribes of Israel, he rebuilt the altar and dug a trench around it. Next he "arranged the wood, cut the bull into pieces and laid it on the wood."

Then, to everybody's surprise, he said, "Fill four large jars with water and pour it on the offering and on the wood."

The water was brought—maybe from the sea, because the springs had all dried up. The men poured it over the altar as Elijah had asked.

Some said, "Does he expect the wood to burn with all that water on it?"

31

But if Elijah heard, he paid no attention. "Do it again," he said, and they did.

"Do it a third time," he said, and the sacrifice was soaked again until water poured into the trench and filled it. Now nobody could say he himself set fire to the sacrifice.

Suddenly a hush fell over the great assembly as Elijah raised his voice in prayer. Everybody listened, even the prophets of Baal, who had stopped shouting.

"O Lord, God of Abraham, Isaac and Israel," he cried aloud, "let it be known today that you are God in Israel and that I am your servant and have done all these things at your com-

HERBERT
RUDEEN

mand. Answer me, O Lord, answer me, so these people will know that you, O Lord, are God, and that you are turning their hearts back again."

Scarcely had he finished praying when there was a flash of flame from the skies. "The fire of the Lord fell and burned up the sacrifice, the wood, the stones and the soil, and also licked up the water in the trench."

It was a marvelous, never-to-be-forgotten sight.

Terrified, the people fell on their faces, crying, "The Lord—he is God; the Lord—he is God!"

They saw what a mistake they had made in worshiping the worthless idols of Baal. From now on they would serve the Lord, the God of Elijah. With their own eyes they had seen His power. Never again would they forget Him.

A Cloud Like a Man's Hand

(1 Kings 18:40-46)

SEEING the people on their knees before God, Elijah gave orders that the prophets of Baal, who had led them into so much wickedness, should be seized and put to death. Nobody lifted a hand to save them. Quickly he led them down to the Kishon Valley and killed them all.

Then he turned to King Ahab, who had watched everything that had happened that day, and said, "Go, eat and drink, for there is the sound of a heavy rain."

Ahab was glad for the chance to eat, but Elijah climbed up to the summit of Carmel again and "bent down to the ground and put his face between his knees." There was nobody on the mountaintop now except the prophet and his servant. The crowds had gone, leaving a great stillness and loneliness.

Bowing low before God, Elijah poured forth his thanks for this day of victory. He thanked God for the swift answer to his prayer, for the flash of fire from heaven, for the defeat of the prophets of Baal, and most of all, for the turning of the hearts of the people back to God.

35

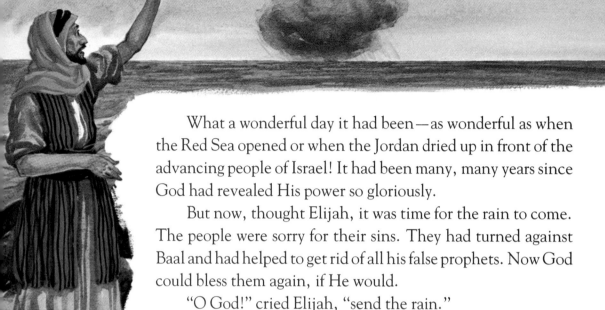

What a wonderful day it had been—as wonderful as when the Red Sea opened or when the Jordan dried up in front of the advancing people of Israel! It had been many, many years since God had revealed His power so gloriously.

But now, thought Elijah, it was time for the rain to come. The people were sorry for their sins. They had turned against Baal and had helped to get rid of all his false prophets. Now God could bless them again, if He would.

"O God!" cried Elijah, "send the rain."

He knew it would come. He was as sure of the rain as he had been of the fire. He had already told Ahab that he had heard the sound of it! But still he prayed.

Raising his head, he said to his servant, "Go and look toward the sea."

The servant obeyed, but soon returned, saying, "There is nothing there."

Again Elijah bowed in prayer, asking even more earnestly for rain. Then he sent his servant a second time to look over the sea. But the sky was still cloudless.

Six times this happened, and yet there was no sign that his prayer had been heard.

But when the servant went the seventh time to look, he

returned excitedly, saying, "A cloud as small as a man's hand is rising from the sea."

That was enough for Elijah. He did not need any other sign. As small as the cloud was—only the size of a man's hand in the great vault of heaven—he was sure it was God's answer. He could almost feel the rain already.

"Hurry!" he said to his servant. "Go and tell Ahab, 'Hitch up your chariot and go down before the rain stops you.' "

As Elijah followed his servant down the mountainside the tiny cloud grew swiftly larger and larger. "The sky grew black with clouds, the wind rose, a heavy rain came on."

The storm and the darkness caught up with Ahab as he fled in his chariot for shelter. The deluge soaked him to the skin, the wild wind tore at his clothing, the crashing thunder frightened his horses as they dashed onward through the night.

Suddenly, as a flash of lightning threw a bright glare across the storm-swept countryside, the worried king saw a figure running ahead of his chariot. Who could it be?

Another flash. Again he glimpsed the figure. The man was still running swiftly and easily, as fast as the horses. Now Ahab recognized him. Elijah! The man of the mountaintop! The man of the fire and the rain! The man of God! Guiding him home through the dark!

"The power of the Lord came upon Elijah and . . . he ran ahead of Ahab all the way to Jezreel." 🖋

The Gentle Whisper

(1 Kings 19:1-18)

ELIJAH must have been very tired after all the excitement of that great day on Carmel, besides running all the way to Jezreel in front of Ahab's chariot. And being so tired, he wasn't ready for the shock that came the next day.

He was still resting when a messenger arrived from Queen Jezebel, who had just heard from Ahab that the prophets of Baal were dead. She had not been on Mount Carmel when the fire fell from heaven.

So she refused to believe that the breaking of the drought had anything to do with Elijah or his God.

Furious that her prophets had been killed, she sent this message: "May the gods deal with me, be it ever so severely, if by this time tomorrow I do not make your life like that of one of them."

Sudden fear seized Elijah. Forgetting that God could care for him just as well in Jezreel as He had by the Kerith Ravine or on the top of Mount Carmel, "Elijah was afraid and ran for his life."

He fled 100 miles from this angry woman. It was not until he

had reached the southern boundary of Judah that he began to feel safe again. Leaving his servant in Beersheba, he went on alone "a day's journey into the desert," and sat down under a broom tree.

By this time Elijah was completely worn out. His spirits were so low that he even prayed that he would die. "Then he lay down under the tree and fell asleep. All at once an angel touched him and said, 'Get up and eat.' " Though Elijah had run from danger, God had not forgotten His weary servant.

Waking, Elijah looked around him and saw "a cake of bread baked over hot coals, and a jar of water. He ate and drank and then lay down again."

How long he slept nobody knows. He was so tired that he might have slept for hours. Then "the angel of the Lord came back a second time and touched him and said, 'Get up and eat, for the journey is too much for you.' "

So Elijah found a second meal waiting for him in the desert. As he ate he must have thanked God that He knew where he was and where he was going. God knew that he would not find any food on the way and that he did not

have enough strength for such a journey.

Gratefully Elijah "ate and drank. Strengthened by that food, he traveled forty days and forty nights until he reached Horeb, the mountain of God."

All his life he had wanted to see Horeb, where so many wonderful things had happened to the children of Israel long ago. He knew it was called "the mountain of God," and he hoped that perhaps he might come closer to God there than he had ever been before.

"My God is the Lord!" he whispered to himself as he journeyed on from day to day over the trackless wilderness. "My God is the Lord! But will I see Him when I reach His mountain? Will I hear His voice?"

At last he arrived and stood in awe upon the historic mountain. Horeb at last! Here, where Moses had stood! Here, where God had spoken alone with His faithful servant when Israel came out of Egypt! Elijah spent the night there in a cave.

Suddenly a strong wind came up, far stronger than the one that had brought the rain to Carmel. It roared up the ravines and churned the dust of the desert into clouds. Picking up huge rocks as if with invisible hands, it dashed them to pieces against the mountainside.

"But the Lord was not in the wind."

Soon the earth began to tremble. Cracks opened in the earth. Elijah had never felt such a quake. "But the Lord was not in the earthquake."

Then the sky glowed as fire burst out on the mountaintop. Elijah remembered the story of how fire and smoke had covered

41

← PAINTING BY MANNING DE V. LEE

Afraid of the threats of the angry queen Jezebel Elijah escaped into the wilderness and wished that he might die, but God sent His angel to encourage His faithful prophet.

the mountain when God gave Israel the Ten Commandments. "But the Lord was not in the fire."

Then where was He?

He was very near, much nearer than Elijah dreamed. In the silence that followed the wind, the earthquake, and the fire, Elijah heard a "gentle whisper." He had thought the mighty God of heaven might be in the hurricane, in the earthquake, or in the raging fire. Yet as he listened to that gentle whisper, he recognized the voice of God.

In reverence "he pulled his cloak over his face and went out and stood at the mouth of the cave."

God asked him one simple question. "What are you doing here, Elijah?"

Elijah had not expected this. He had come all this way to talk with God and worship Him, not to answer questions. But he knew what God meant. He knew God was saying to him, "Why aren't you in Jezreel standing for Me before that wicked Jezebel? Why did you not stay and follow up the victory I gave you on Carmel?"

"I am the only one left," Elijah said, "and now they are trying to kill me too."

42

"No," God said to him. "I reserve seven thousand in Israel—all whose knees have not bowed down to Baal." The suggestion was, "*They* haven't run away."

Then God told him to go back to his work in Israel. On his way he was to anoint Hazael to be king over Aram, Jehu to be king over Israel, and a man named Elisha to take his place as the prophet of the Lord.

As he journeyed northward toward Damascus Elijah thought again and again of what had happened at Horeb. That gentle whisper had moved the prophet more than everything else he had seen or heard on the mountain. It had stirred him more than all the excitement on Mount Carmel, when fire fell from heaven and the prophets of Baal were put to death.

Elijah had often seen God show His majesty and power, sometimes to protect His people, sometimes to remind them that the Lord should be approached with proper reverence and respect. But now he had been shown an even greater power, the power of simple words of truth, even when spoken in a gentle whisper.

When we are reverently willing to listen, our Heavenly Father would much rather speak to us in this way. As God would explain later to the prophet Zechariah, " 'Not by might nor by power, but by my Spirit,' says the Lord Almighty." *

---

* Zechariah 4:6.

The Stolen Vineyard

(1 Kings 21:1-26)

KING AHAB was a very rich man, as wealth was counted in his day. He owned at least two palaces, one in Samaria and one in Jezreel. The one in Samaria was a "palace he built and inlaid with ivory." Its walls were decorated with polished ivory carved from the tusks of elephants.

But in spite of all his riches, Ahab was not a happy man. Like many boys and girls today, he was always wanting more. If someone had something better than he had, he felt envious and miserable.

One day, as he was looking out of the window of his palace in Jezreel, he noticed a beautiful vineyard next to the royal lands. The thought occurred to him that it would make a fine addition to the palace gardens, and he made up his mind to buy it.

Going to Naboth, the owner, he offered to give him another vineyard in exchange for this one or, if he preferred, to pay whatever it was worth.

THE STOLEN VINEYARD

It was a fair enough offer, but Naboth didn't want to sell. The vineyard had been his father's, he said, and his grandfather's. It had belonged to his family for more years than he could tell, and he couldn't bring himself to part with it.

Ahab was very upset, and when he got back to his palace he behaved like a spoiled child. Throwing himself on his bed, he turned his face to the wall and refused to eat.

When he didn't come down to dinner that evening, Queen Jezebel went to his room to find out what was the matter.

"Why are you so sullen?" she asked. "Why won't you eat?"

Then he told her how he had offered to buy Naboth's vineyard and the man had refused to sell it.

Jezebel scoffed. "That's a fine thing to be miserable about!"

she said. "Aren't you king? Can't you do what you like? Get up! Eat and be happy! If you want that vineyard, I'll get it for you."

Ahab did as he was told, and Jezebel set about getting the vineyard for him in her own wicked way.

She wrote to the heads of the city council and told them to "proclaim a day of fasting and seat Naboth in a prominent place among the people." Then they were to call in two false witnesses who would testify that Naboth had blasphemed God and the king. After hearing the evidence, they were to find Naboth guilty and have him stoned to death.

It was as simple as that, and as evil. With all the city officials already sold out to Jezebel and afraid for their lives, poor Naboth didn't have a chance.

The court was summoned. The two witnesses came in and accused Naboth of blasphemy. He said he was innocent, but it was no use. He swore he had never uttered blasphemy in all his life, either against God or the king, but nobody listened to him. The judges accepted the lies of the two witnesses and condemned him to death. He was then carried out of the city and stoned.

But if Jezebel and Ahab thought they were going to get away with this wicked murder, they were mistaken. The very day Ahab walked into Naboth's vineyard to take possession of it, who should be there but Elijah. Ahab had last seen Elijah running before his chariot on that stormy night after fire had fallen from heaven on Mount Carmel and the prophets of Baal had been killed.

"So you have found me, my enemy!" he cried in a startled voice.

"I have found you," replied Elijah, sternly: "because you have sold yourself to do evil in the eyes of the Lord."

"This is what the Lord says: 'Have you not murdered a man and seized his property? . . . In the place where dogs licked up Naboth's blood, dogs will lick up your blood—yes, yours!' "

Concerning Jezebel, he said, "Dogs will devour Jezebel by the wall of Jezreel."

Elijah could not have spoken more frankly, and Ahab was left in no doubt as to what God thought of the murder of Naboth. We may be sure that he never got one moment's pleasure out of that stolen vineyard. Every time he walked in it, he must have wondered whether Elijah was hiding somewhere among the vines, waiting to condemn him again for his evil deed. Every time he looked at it from his palace window he must have thought of the price both he and Jezebel would have to pay for it someday.

That is what the bitter fruit of envy, jealousy, and selfishness is like.

Elijah's Prophecy Comes True

(1 Kings 21:27-22:40; 2 Kings 9:33-37)

AHAB did not live very long after he stole Naboth's vineyard. He was sorry for his sin, but he could neither give the vineyard back to the dead man nor forget the great wrong he had done.

Some time later Jehoshaphat, king of Judah, came on a state visit to Samaria. A great feast was held in honor of the occasion. The two kings, dressed in their royal robes, sat on thrones placed outside the city gate. They talked of many things, but mostly about the city of Ramoth Gilead which, Ahab said, belonged to Israel but was now occupied by the Arameans. Would Jehoshaphat help him get it back?

"I am as you are, my people as your people, my horses as your horses," said Jehoshaphat with great courtesy. "But don't you think we ought to ask the Lord about it?"

Ahab called for his "prophets." They came, hundreds of them, and said exactly what he wanted them to say: "Go, . . . for the Lord will give it into the king's hand."

One man even put iron horns on his head and said, "This

is what the Lord says: 'With these you will gore the Arameans until they are destroyed.' "

But Jehoshaphat didn't like the look of these men. "Is there not a prophet of the Lord here, whom we can inquire of?" he said.

"There is still one man," said Ahab testily, "through whom we can inquire of the Lord, but I hate him because he never prophesies anything good about me, but always bad."

"Don't say that," said Jehoshaphat. "Call him."

So Micaiah was called, and speaking in the name of the Lord, he warned that the plan would fail.

"I saw all Israel scattered on the hills like sheep without a shepherd," he said.

"There," said Ahab to Jehoshaphat. "Didn't I tell you that he never prophesies anything good about me, but only bad?"

"Your prophets are lying," said Micaiah. "The Lord has decreed disaster for you."

At this, the man wearing the iron horns slapped Micaiah on the cheek, and Ahab said, "Put this fellow in prison and give him nothing but bread and water until I return safely."

As the soldiers led him away, Micaiah cried, "If you ever return safely, the Lord has not spoken through me."

Ahab didn't want to hear the truth, and he persuaded Jehoshaphat to go along with him. The two kings marched on Ramoth Gilead, but their armies were defeated and scattered like sheep without a shepherd, just as Micaiah had said.

Jehoshaphat escaped with his life, but Ahab was killed. "Someone drew his bow at random and hit the king of Israel between the sections of his armor," wounding him seriously.

Ahab's servants propped him up so that it would look as though he were still fighting, but so much blood poured from his wound that it covered the bottom of his chariot, and he died at sundown that evening.

They brought the dead king back to Samaria and buried him there. As Ahab's chariot and armor were being washed in the pool of Samaria, dogs came and licked up his blood.

Elijah's prophecy was fulfilled.

As for Jezebel, she lived 11 years after Ahab's death. But the day came when her own guards threw her out of the window of the palace in Jezreel, where she once had plotted the death of Naboth. "Some of her blood spattered the wall and the horses." Afterward, when they came to bury her, "they found nothing except her skull, her feet and her hands." The dogs had eaten the rest of her, just as Elijah long years before had said they would.

It is good to remember that God always means what He says. His prophecies and His promises always come to pass. 🖋

Fate of the Three Captains

(1 Kings 22:40, 51-53; 2 Kings 1)

AFTER Ahab's death his son Ahaziah became king of Israel. Unfortunately, he was no better than his father or his mother. He "served and worshiped Baal and provoked the Lord, the God of Israel, to anger."

One day he fell out of an upper window in the palace. Apparently the wooden lattice gave way as he leaned against it. We don't know how badly he was hurt, but it was enough to make him worry whether or not he would get better.

Anxious to learn his fate, he sent messengers to ask Baal-Zebub, the god of Ekron, just as though this wooden idol would know what was going to happen to him.

On their way the messengers met Elijah, though they did not recognize him. He asked them sternly why they were going to ask for help from Baal-Zebub rather than from the God of heaven. Then he ordered them to turn back and tell Ahaziah that he was going to die. The messengers were so frightened by the old prophet that they obeyed him.

Ahaziah was surprised to see them back so soon. When

51

they told him what had happened, he asked them to describe the man who had spoken to them.

"He was a man with a garment of hair," they said, "and with a leather belt around his waist." They did not need to say more.

"That was Elijah the Tishbite!" said Ahaziah. He sent one of his captains with 50 men to seize Elijah and bring him to Samaria.

The captain found the prophet sitting on a hilltop and ordered him to come down at once. "Man of God," he cried, "the king says, 'Come down!' "

Elijah refused. He felt that this was no way for these godless soldiers of a godless king to treat the prophet of the Lord.

"If I am a man of God," he said, "may fire come down from heaven and consume you and your fifty men!" A moment later a sudden blaze of fire fell from heaven, and the men vanished.

When the king heard what had happened, he was outraged and sent a second captain with another 50 men to capture Elijah and bring him to court.

Elijah was still on the hilltop, quite undisturbed.

"Come down at once!" ordered the captain of the second fifty. "King's orders!"

Once again Elijah said, "If I am a man of God, . . . may fire come down from heaven and consume you and your fifty men!"

52

Again fire fell from heaven, and the captain and his men were consumed.

When news of this reached Ahaziah he sent a third captain with 50 men to take Elijah. This captain, however, had learned something from the sad fate of his friends. When he came to the hill where Elijah was sitting he "fell on his knees before Elijah. 'Man of God,' he begged, 'please have respect for my life and the lives of these fifty men, your servants!' "

God appreciated the humble attitude of this man, and the respect he paid to His prophet. "Go down with him," He told Elijah. "Do not be afraid of him."

So Elijah went with this captain and his 50 men and came to the palace where Ahaziah was lying in bed. Elijah showed no fear, though he was now within the king's power and could easily have been thrown into a dungeon any minute. He did not change his message either.

Instead, he told the king, as he had already told his messengers, that because he asked for help from Baal-Zebub, the god of Ekron, rather from the God of heaven, he would not get well. He would die.

Ahaziah did die, just as Elijah had said. He died not only because he had tried to ask Baal-Zebub for help, but because all his life—just like his father and mother—he had hated the Lord and served the gods of the heathen.

Heaven's Fiery Chariot

(2 Kings 2:1-15)

ELIJAH'S work was almost done. He had stood for God the best he knew how in a very evil time. Bravely he had fought God's battles and championed His cause. In his heart he felt that God was about to call him away from this world.

Elisha was with him constantly now, for Elijah was helping the young man get ready to take over his work when he had to leave it. Elisha, you remember, was mentioned by the "gentle whisper" as the one to take Elijah's place. Elijah had anointed him on his return from Mount Horeb, and the two had been working together ever since.

As they approached Bethel, a "group of prophets" (TEV) came out to meet them. These were young men from one of the schools of the prophets Elijah is believed to have started.

Strangely, these young people had the same idea about Elijah—that he would not be around much longer. They asked Elisha if God was going to take his master away soon.

"Yes, I know, . . . but do not speak of it," he said to them.

He did not want to talk about it.

Then Elijah told Elisha to wait at Bethel while he went on by himself. "The Lord has sent me to Jericho," he said.

Elisha refused to let him go alone. "As surely as the Lord lives and as you live," he said, "I will not leave you."

So the two went on together to Jericho, where there was another group of prophets. Here again the young men came out to meet them, and they also warned Elisha that he would soon be losing his master.

"Yes, I know," he said to them, "but do not speak of it."

Elijah told Elisha to wait at Jericho while he went on over Jordan, but again Elisha refused. He had made up his mind to stay with his master to the very end, not knowing when or how that would be. "As surely as the Lord lives and as you live, I will not leave you," he said.

So the two went on toward Jordan, while at least 50 young men from the company followed at a distance to see what might happen.

They saw plenty. When Elijah and Elisha reached the river, they did not wait for a boat to ferry them across. Taking off his cloak, Elijah "rolled it up and struck the water with it. The water divided to the right and to the left, and the two of them crossed over on dry ground."

If the young people thought that they might follow, they were mistaken, for the water quickly flowed together again. A

moment later the Jordan looked the same as ever.

On the other side, Elijah turned to Elisha and said very tenderly, "Tell me, what can I do for you before I am taken from you?"

The dreaded moment of parting had come! Soon Elijah would be gone forever. What should Elisha ask for? Money? Land? Houses? Position? He could have asked for anything, for he was sure Elijah was going straight to heaven.

" 'Let me inherit a double portion of your spirit,' Elisha replied."

He could not have made a better choice. God must have been as pleased with him as He had been with Solomon when he had asked for wisdom.

Elijah said he had asked for something that was hard to give—for of course only God could give His Spirit. But he added, "If you see me when I am taken from you, it will be yours."

The Bible says, "They were walking along and talking together." It is a pity we do not know the last precious words these two great men of God said to each other. No doubt Elijah urged Elisha to be true and loyal to God and keep the good work going which he had started.

By now they were not far from Pisgah, which is just 10 miles from Jericho. Perhaps they even climbed to the top, to the place where Moses died and God raised him from the dead.

The wind began to blow—harder and harder, with a twisting, swirling motion. Elijah seemed to be caught up in it and lifted above the earth. Suddenly a blaze of light surrounded them as something appeared in the sky, like one of Ahab's chariots, only 10,000 times more glorious.

It was shining as radiantly as if it were on fire, while the creatures that pulled it seemed to be on fire too. Surely it must be one of God's own chariots, a chariot of angels, sent to bring his faithful servant home! Swiftly it approached Elijah, who stepped into it and was gone.

"And Elijah went up to heaven in a whirlwind."

"My father, my father!" cried Elisha as he saw his beloved master carried swiftly upward in this blaze of glory. "The chariots and horsemen of Israel!"

Something fell from the chariot as it sped away. Slowly it billowed down to earth as the wind subsided. Eagerly Elisha ran to pick it up. It was a cloak, Elijah's cloak, the

prophet's last gift to his friend.

Picking it up, Elisha returned to the Jordan. Beyond the river was Jericho with its group of prophets, and beyond that, the great work God wanted him to do throughout all Israel.

Could he do this work? Was he prepared for it? Could he be the leader Elijah had been? Would God give him the double portion of His Spirit he had asked for?

The Jordan was his first test. Would it open for him as it had for Elijah? Taking Elijah's cloak, he hit the water as his master had done, crying, "Where now is the Lord, the God of Elijah?" The river parted and Elisha went over. Now he knew for sure that God was with him and always would be.

The group of prophets was watching. At first they thought Elijah had returned. But no, Elisha was alone. Then they knew they had a new master. "The spirit of Elijah is resting on Elisha," they said.

And they were right. Elisha went on to do more and greater miracles than even Elijah had done. 🖋

PART TWO

Stories of

Elisha

(2 Kings 2:16-13:20)

Bad Boys and the Bears

(2 Kings 2:16-24)

ELISHA did his best to explain what had happened to Elijah, but people wouldn't believe him. Even the young men in the group of prophets at Jericho found it hard to understand how their beloved master could have been taken up to heaven in a chariot of fire and a whirlwind. They were sure that even if God had taken him up, He must have set him down again somewhere, maybe "on some mountain or in some valley." They wanted to go and search for him.

Elisha told them not to, for they would only waste their time. But they went anyway, all 50 of them. For three days they hunted for Elijah without success.

One day the elders of the city of Jericho came to Elisha and asked him if he could do something about their water supply. It had a bad taste, they said, and was not good for irrigation. Plants watered with it wouldn't grow.

Elisha was glad to help. He called for a new bowl full of salt and took it to the place where the spring bubbled out of the ground. Pouring in the salt, he said, "This is what the Lord says:

When the water of the city of Jericho became bitter and unfit for use, Elisha called for some salt which he poured into the source of the stream, and God made the water good to drink.

'I have healed this water. Never again will it cause death or make the land unproductive.' And the water has remained wholesome to this day."

That stream is still flowing, and the water is still sweet. I know, for I drank some of it one day when visiting there some years ago.

Leaving the people of Jericho very happy, Elisha made his way back to Bethel. To his surprise, a group of unruly boys came running toward him as he approached the city. They shouted, "Go on up, you baldhead! . . . Go on up, you baldhead!"

So his story of Elijah's translation had reached here already! And this was what the people thought of it! Clearly they didn't believe a word of his report. They were laughing at the idea of anyone going up to heaven in a fiery chariot. These rude youngsters were actually telling him to go up there, too.

Elisha saw that it was all part of a plan to wreck his work. His enemies wanted to make him the object of everyone's jokes. He could not permit it. And he could not allow such a solemn,

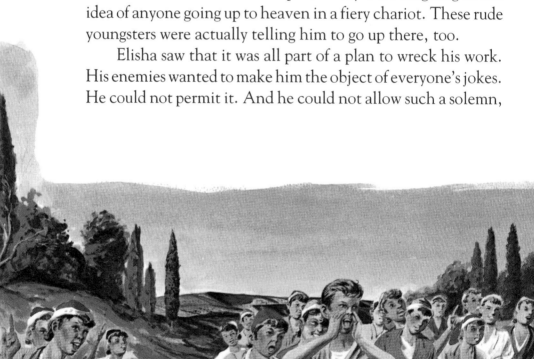

beautiful event as his master's triumphal entry into heaven to be laughed at, either. This was too much. These bad boys must be taught a lesson.

As the crowd of scoffing youngsters followed him chanting, "Go on up, you baldhead," Elisha "turned around, looked at them and called down a curse on them in the name of the Lord." In other words, he asked God to deal with them as He saw fit.

As he did, two bears came out of the nearby woods. Suddenly the mocking stopped, and laughter turned to screams of terror as the boys fled for their lives. But the bears caught up with them and mauled 42 of them. How badly they were hurt we are not told, but it is safe to say they all learned a lesson that day which they never forgot. Never again would they treat a man of God with disrespect.

Elisha went on to Mount Carmel, where God had come so near to his master, and fire had fallen from heaven. It was a good place to go to at the beginning of his ministry.

Valley of Red Ditches

(2 Kings 2:25-3:24)

FROM Mount Carmel Elisha went to Samaria. He traveled a great deal, just as Elijah had done before him, not stopping very long in any one place.

One day there was a loud knocking on the door of the humble home where he was staying. Going to see who was there, Elisha found a crowd of armed men outside. Among them were two royal figures in fine armor.

He recognized them at once. The old, bearded man was Jehoshaphat, king of Judah. The other was young Joram, king of Israel, who had become king when his brother Ahaziah fell out of the palace window and died from his injuries. A son of Ahab, he was as wicked as his father. The two kings said that they had come to talk with Elisha about an important matter.

Suddenly turning on Joram, Elisha asked what he meant by coming to a prophet of the Lord. "Go to your own prophets!" he said to him, "the prophets of your father and mother."

"If it were not for the presence of Jehoshaphat, king of

Judah," he added, "I wouldn't even look at you or see you."

It was hardly a tactful way to talk to a king, but Elisha was a very brave man, and he wanted Joram to know that he strongly disapproved of his evil ways. But because good King Jehoshaphat was there, Elisha agreed to listen to their story.

They were both in great trouble. Their armies had started out to fight the Moabites. Thinking to surprise them by attacking from the east, they had taken a long detour through desert country and now were out of water. There was nothing to drink either for the men or the animals . They were at the mercy of their enemies. What should they do now? Did Elisha have anything to suggest?

Elisha called for a harpist, and while he listened to the sweet music, "the hand of the Lord came upon Elisha and he said, 'This is what the Lord says: Make this valley full of ditches. For this is what the Lord says: 'You will see neither wind nor rain, yet this valley will be filled with water, and you, your cattle and your other animals will drink. This is an easy thing in the eyes of the Lord; he will also hand Moab over to you.' "

I can almost hear Joram scoffing, "Dig ditches in a dry valley! What an idea!" But Jehoshaphat believed God's prophet,

and the ditches were dug. Those ditches proved his faith.

Early the next morning the sun rose in a cloudless sky. The air was still, and there was no sign of rain. But suddenly down one of the mountain ravines "from the direction of Edom" came a raging stream of water. It spread over the valley floor and filled the ditches to overflowing. Soldiers, horses, and cattle drank greedily, and their strength revived.

By this time, of course, the Moabites were awake and ready for battle. Looking eastward, they saw the soldiers of Israel behaving in a very strange way. Some were standing, others were kneeling, and still others were lying flat on their stomachs. And it looked as if blood was all around them, because the early morning sun was reflected from the water-filled ditches.

"Look! They are killing one another!" they cried, and dashed down the mountainside to finish off the invaders of their country.

Of course they had made a dreadful mistake. When they reached the ditches, they found they were full of water, not blood. Maybe some of them fell into the ditches and were drowned. Anyway, the Israelites had seen them coming and were ready for them.

Thanks to the God of Elisha, what might have been a bad defeat was turned into a great victory.

Mother's Mysterious Oil Pots

(2 Kings 4:1-7)

ABOUT this time one of the group of prophets died, leaving a widow with two young sons. The Bible doesn't tell us the boys' names, so I am sure nobody will mind if I call them Jonas and Joel.

The little family was so poor that there was no money in the house. Worse than that, their father had been heavily in debt, and now the creditor wanted his money.

Their mother told the creditor she couldn't give him what he asked for; she just didn't have it. So he said he would take Jonas and Joel and sell them as slaves to pay the bill.

Poor little Mother! How sad and frightened she must have been! But what could she do? Where could she turn for help? Then she thought of Elisha.

Leaving the two boys at home, she went looking for the prophet, hoping against hope that he would show her a way out of her trouble. At last she found him and told her story.

"Tell me," said Elisha kindly, "what do you have in your house?"

"Nothing," said the poor widow. "Nothing, that is, except a jar of oil."

Then Elisha told her to do a strange thing. "Go around and ask all your neighbors for empty jars. Don't ask for just a few."

He must have noticed the questioning look on the widow's face, for he went on to tell her what to do with the empty oil jars. After she had gathered all she could find, she was to shut the door of her house and start pouring oil from her jar into the empty containers. And she was to keep on pouring until all the jars were full.

The widow must have wondered for a moment whether the man of God was serious. She knew she had just one jar of oil, and how could that one jar fill many empty jars? And what would the neighbors think if she started asking them for all their crockery?

On the way home she must have questioned whether or not she should do as Elisha had said. Nobody likes to look silly before friends, and this could make her appear very foolish indeed if it didn't work. Imagine the kitchen floor covered with empty oil jars, and nothing happening to them!

She decided she would do as she had been told and trust the God of Elisha. "Jonas," she said, when she reached home, "please go next door and ask Mrs. Isaacson for a couple of empty oil jars; and Joel, you go up the road

and ask Mrs. Naomi for all she can spare."

"Why, Mother?"

"Never mind, dears.
Go and get them. Then ask all the other neighbors for
every jar they will let me have."

As the boys ran off they must have wondered what was
happening to Mother. Perhaps the worry of Father's death had
been too much for her. But they asked for the jars anyway. Soon
they were back, carrying all the jars they could hold. Then they
ran off for more.

The neighbors, looking out of their windows, began to
wonder what was going on. "Why are those boys taking all
those oil jars down to their house?" they asked themselves. But
when they asked Jonas and Joel, the only answer they got was,
"Don't know; Mother just wants them for something."

When the kitchen floor was just about covered with jars,
Mother shut the door.

"What are you going to do with all of them?" asked Jonas
and Joel, amused.

"Never mind; just watch and see." Mother picked up her

71

one precious jar with the oil in it. With a prayer in her heart, "Dear God, make it work!" she began to pour.

The first jar wasn't too big a worry, for she was just pouring from one to another. But the second! She felt her own jar; it was still heavy. She looked into it; there was still some oil there. She began to pour into the second jar. Soon it too was filled to the brim. Eagerly she turned to the third jar, the fourth, the fifth, the sixth. Then she lost count.

With their eyes popping out, the boys looked on in amazement.

"But where's it coming from, Mother?"

"I don't know!" she cried as she went on pouring. "I don't know!"

Row after row of jars was filled. Suddenly she noticed that she had reached the last jar.

"Jonas, Joel!" she cried. "More jars! Get me another jar quickly!"

But there were no jars left.

"Then the oil stopped flowing."

Leaving the boys to look after the precious oil, Mother ran to Elisha and gasped out her wonderful story, her heart overflowing with gratitude to God for His goodness.

There must have been a lovely smile on Elisha's face as he listened. Then he said to her, "Go, sell the oil and pay your debts. You and your sons can live on what is left."

God loves to do things like this for those who trust Him.

73

With her heart overflowing to God for His goodness, the poor widow began pouring the oil into the vessels as Elisha had told her, and it continued to flow until every jar was full.

Kindness Repaid

(2 Kings 4:8-37)

AS ELISHA journeyed here and there through Palestine he often passed through a place called Shunem, where a very wealthy lady lived. Sometimes he stopped at her home and asked for something to eat. He was always invited in and well fed, and always he left a blessing behind him when he went on his way.

Elisha impressed the great lady very much. He was so courteous, so friendly, so reverent, so different from men of the world, that she said to her husband one day, "I know that this man who often comes our way is a holy man of God." She suggested that they build a little room where he could rest, and put "a bed and a table, a chair and a lamp" inside.

Her husband agreed. They built and furnished the room, and the next time Elisha arrived, they invited him to spend the night. How pleased and thankful he was! Nobody had ever been so kind to him before.

The next day Elisha told his servant Gehazi to tell the lady that he wanted to express his gratitude. "Tell her, 'You have gone to all this trouble for us. Now what can be done for you?' "

He offered to speak to the king or the commander of the army for her, if she had any favor to ask of them. But she said No, she was content. Then he said to Gehazi, "What *can* we do for her?"

Gehazi thought it over. Soon he came up with a bright idea. "She has no son and her husband is old," he said.

"Aha!" said Elisha, grateful for the suggestion. "Call her."

When the lady came, Elisha promised that before a year had passed she would have a son.

"Impossible!" she said.

But nothing is impossible with God. At the very time Elisha said, the little boy was born. The lady loved her son very dearly and watched over him night and day as he grew

up. Elisha must have taken a lot of interest in him too as he visited the family from time to time.

Then one hot summer day, when the boy was out in the harvest field with his father, he suddenly cried out, "My head! My head!" Perhaps he had sunstroke. Anyway, his father became very worried and said to one of his servants, "Carry him to his mother."

She took him on her lap and held him until noon, when he died. Then she carried the limp little boy upstairs to the room she had made for Elisha and laid him on the bed. Closing the door behind her, she went out with aching heart and tear-drenched face.

But she wiped away the tears, and putting on a brave face, she asked her husband for a servant and one of the donkeys so she could visit Elisha.

He wanted to know why. "It's not the New Moon or the Sabbath," he said.

But she didn't tell him why, perhaps because the shock would be too great if he found out his little son was dead. Saddling the donkey herself, she said to the servant, "Lead on; don't slow down for me unless I tell you."

They rode at full speed to Mount Carmel, where they found Elisha. Falling at his feet, she told him what had happened and about the cold little form that lay on his bed.

Elisha was shocked. Handing his staff to Gehazi, he told him to hurry to the dead child and lay the staff on his face. Gehazi ran on ahead, and Elisha followed, the anxious mother at his side.

Soon the two saw Gehazi returning, looking sad and worried.

"The boy has not awakened," he said.

Elisha was worried now. Arriving at the house, he went upstairs, entered his room, "shut the door," and "prayed to the Lord." What a prayer that was! How he must have implored the great and wonderful God whom he served to honor his faith and restore the little boy to life!

"Then he got on the bed and lay upon the boy, mouth to mouth, eyes to eyes, hands to hands. As he stretched himself out upon him, the boy's body grew warm." But there was no other sign of life.

Elisha got up from the bed and "walked back and forth in the room," wondering what more he could do. But his faith was still strong that God could raise the dead—and would. As he paced up and down he prayed more and more urgently that God would do this wonderful thing for the glory of His name and the blessing of this dear woman who had been so kind to him.

Then he went back to the bed. The little lad still lay motionless. He stretched himself on top of him once more. Suddenly the child awoke, sneezed seven times, and opened his eyes.

The miracle had happened!

Calling the mother, Elisha said kindly, with deep happiness in his voice, "Take your son."

Overjoyed, she fell at the prophet's feet and poured out her thanks. Then she picked up her boy, hugging and kissing him as only a mother can who has just seen her dearest treasure brought back from the dead.

Faithful Little Maid

(2 Kings 5:1-15)

L ET ME go! Let me go!" screamed the little girl. "Don't take me away from my mother!"

But the cruel raiders took no notice of her cries. They threw her on a horse behind a big, burly Aramean soldier and set out for Damascus.

Weeping all the way, the little girl sobbed out between her tears, "Why did God let this happen to me? Why? Why? Why?"

In the big city she was sold as a slave and became the servant of the wife of Naaman, "commander of the army of the king of Aram."

How homesick and hopeless she must have felt that first night in the big house, with all those strange people! Yet she didn't forget to say her prayers. Her parents had brought her up to love the God of heaven, and she made up her mind she would be true to Him whatever might happen.

Fortunately her mistress was kind to her. Soon they were talking together like mother and daughter. Perhaps the little

maid told some of the stories her real mother had told her about the wonderful way the God of heaven had cared for Israel in years gone by. She might have told about crossing the Red Sea or how God provided "bread from heaven" in the desert — stories every Hebrew child knew by heart.

Often the little maid noticed that her mistress had a very sad look on her face. She wondered why, but didn't dare to ask. Then one day she found out what the trouble was. Naaman, her master, had that most dreaded disease, leprosy.

The little maid had seen lepers before, and she knew the awful things the disease did to them. Her kind heart went out in sympathy to her master and mistress. She longed to do something to help them, but what could a little girl do, so far from home in a strange, strange land?

Then she had a bright idea. If *she* couldn't help, maybe God could. Seeing her mistress in tears, she went to her and said, very gently, "If only my master would see the prophet who is in Samaria! He would cure him of his leprosy."

80

"Sweet child, what makes you think that?" asked her mistress.

This gave the little maid her chance. She began to talk about all the wonderful things Elisha had done, and Elijah before him.

"Why, once Elisha raised a dead boy to life. Yes, he was quite dead. Everybody says so. And another time he made the water from the bitter spring of Jericho taste sweet. His master, Elijah, did some wonderful things too. He made a poor widow's jar of flour and jar of oil last many days, maybe a whole year.

"Once he even brought fire down from heaven on the top of Mount Carmel and burned up the sacrifice, even though it was soaking wet with water. Oh, yes, my lady, the God of heaven is a wonderful God. And Elisha is His prophet, a man of God. I'm sure he would heal your husband if he'd just go to see him."

The little maid talked on and on. Her mistress was so touched that she told the whole story to a servant, who went and told it to Naaman. He was so impressed that he told the king of Aram. The king thought the child had a fine idea, and said he would write to the king of Israel about it at once.

Unfortunately the king of Aram got things a bit mixed up. By the time the little maid's story reached him, he thought it was the king of Israel, not Elisha, who was to do the healing, and he put this in his letter. He wrote: "I am sending my servant Naaman to you so that you may cure him of his leprosy."

When the king of Israel received the letter and learned that Naaman had already arrived with "ten talents [750 pounds, or 340 kilograms] of silver, six thousand shekels [150 pounds, or 68 kilograms] of gold and ten sets of clothing" to pay for his cure, he almost went out of his mind. The Bible says he tore his clothes and cried out, "Am I God? Can I kill and bring back to life? Why does this fellow send someone to me to be cured of his leprosy? See how he is trying to pick a quarrel with me!"

Soon the story was all over Samaria. It reached Elisha,

who must have smiled at the fix the idolatrous king was in. Elisha could have left him to find his own way out, but seeing an opportunity to bring glory to God in a foreign land, he told the king to send Naaman to him.

"So Naaman went with his horses and chariots and stopped at the door of Elisha's house."

Elisha sent a messenger to say that if he would wash in the river Jordan seven times, he would be cured of his leprosy.

This made Naaman very angry, and he rode away, saying to his servants, "I thought that he would surely come out to me and stand and call on the name of the Lord his God, wave his hand over the spot and cure me of my leprosy."

He was upset because Elisha had not made a fuss over him—and worse, because his national pride had been hurt. Why should he go and wash in the Jordan? "Are not Abana and Pharpar, the rivers of Damascus, better than any of the waters of Israel?" he snapped. "Couldn't I wash in *them* and be cleansed?"

His servants had more sense. They said to him, "If the prophet had asked you to do some big thing, wouldn't you have done it? Why not obey him when he suggests something as simple as washing yourself?"

At last Naaman agreed. Turning his chariot around, he drove down toward the Jordan. It was a rough, bumpy journey, and many times he must have wondered whether it was worthwhile. Perhaps, after all, the prophet was

just playing with him because he was a foreign general.

Arriving at the Jordan, he took off his clothes and waded in, while his servants watched to see what would happen. Then he dipped under the water. Everyone looked at the white spot that marked the place where the leprosy had started. It was still there.

He dipped under the water the second time. Still nothing happened. He went in the third time, the fourth, the fifth, the sixth, and still the horrid mark was there.

All the servants had been counting. Everyone knew that the next time would be the seventh and the last.

Once more Naaman dipped under the water. "Look! Look!" he cried. "It's gone!"

All the servants crowded around. It was true. The leprosy had disappeared.

Throwing on his clothes, Naaman leaped into his chariot. How he drove up that mountain road! It's a wonder the wheels didn't come off as they sank in the ruts and bumped against the rocks. His servants followed at the same wild speed, until they all arrived at Elisha's house.

This time Elisha was there to greet them, for he guessed what had happened when he heard the galloping hoofs. Scarcely knowing how to express his gratitude, Naaman bowed his head and said, "Now I know that there is no God in all the world except in Israel."

The little captive servant girl had not only saved her master's life but she had helped him learn to worship God. How happy she must have been when she heard the news!

85

← PAINTING BY HARRY ANDERSON

The leprosy of Naaman, captain of the host of the king of Syria, was cured when he obeyed the word of the Lord through Elisha and washed himself seven times in the Jordan.

Greedy Gehazi

(2 Kings 5:15-27)

NAAMAN was so happy and thankful that he had been cured of his leprosy that he wanted to give Elisha all the gold, silver, and beautiful garments he had brought with him.

But Elisha wanted no payment for something God had done. He hoped that this famous general would go back to his king and country and tell how the God of Israel, unlike the gods of the heathen, is willing to help the needy of all nations free of charge, "without money and without cost." *

"As surely as the Lord lives, whom I serve," he said to Naaman, "I will not accept a thing."

Naaman urged him, but he again refused.

Aglow with the memory of this wonderful generosity, Naaman started back for Damascus. No doubt he said to his servants, "I never saw anything like this in all my life. Imagine a man refusing all that money I offered him! The God he serves must be different from any I ever heard about." The happy party moved northward, everyone eager to get home and tell all they had seen and heard in Israel.

Just then something made Naaman look back. A man was running after them. From a distance he looked like Gehazi, Elisha's servant. What could he want? Naaman reined in his horses, and everybody else did the same. Gehazi came up panting, and Naaman got out of his chariot to greet him. "Is everything all right?" he asked, a little worried.

"Oh, yes," said Gehazi cheerfully, and then he made up the biggest lie of his life. "Everything is all right. . . . My master sent me to say, 'Two young men from the company of the prophets have just come to me from the hill country of Ephraim. Please give them a talent [75 pounds, or 34 kilograms] of silver and two sets of clothing.' "

The story sounded perfectly plausible, and Naaman was eager to give even more than Gehazi had asked. "Take *two* talents," he said. "He urged Gehazi to accept them, and then tied up the two talents of silver in two bags, with two sets of clothing. He gave them to two of his servants, and they carried them ahead of Gehazi."

Naaman started up his horses again and drove off, wondering whether Gehazi's story was true or whether Elisha really wanted the money for himself after all.

Gehazi returned to Elisha's house and hid his loot in a secret place. But if he thought he was going to keep anything

like this secret, he just didn't know his master.

"Where have you been?" asked Elisha as he entered the house again.

"Nowhere."

"Nowhere!" exclaimed the prophet in great anger. "Was not my spirit with you when the man got down from his chariot to meet you?"

Gehazi looked at the floor, ashamed. He had been found out! His awful lies were known!

But Elisha was not finished with him. "Is this the time to take money, or to accept clothes, olive groves, vineyards, flocks, herds, or menservants and maidservants?" he asked sternly.

It was not. Gehazi, as the servant of God's prophet, should have known it.

Then came his punishment: "Naaman's leprosy will cling to you and to your descendants forever. Then Gehazi went from Elisha's presence and he was leprous, as white as snow."

By his greed, selfishness, and falsehood, Gehazi had spoiled something very beautiful that God had tried to do for the whole kingdom of Aram and all the world beyond.

---

* Isaiah 55:1.

Elisha's Secret Army

(2 Kings 6:8-23)

SOME time after Naaman's return to Damascus, the king of Aram—for some reason we do not know—declared war on Israel again. But something went wrong with his campaign. Every time he planned an attack or an ambush, the king of Israel heard about it and prepared for it.

This happened so many times that the king of Aram was sure he had a traitor among his men. Sending for his officers, he said to them angrily, "Will you not tell me which of us is on the side of the king of Israel?"

" 'None of us, my lord the king,' said one of his officers, 'but Elisha, the prophet who is in Israel, tells the king of Israel the very words you speak in your bedroom.' "

It could have been Naaman himself who said this, or someone to whom he had spoken about the power of Elisha's God.

Now the problem seemed easy to the king. All he had to do was get Elisha, and his problems would be over. So he said to his men, " 'Go, find out where he is, . . . so I can send men and capture him.'

"The report came back: 'He is in Dothan.' "

So the king ordered "horses, and chariots, and a strong force" to go to Dothan to fetch this man who knew too much. Thinking to take Elisha by surprise, the army arrived by night and completely surrounded the city. There seemed no way of escape for the man of God.

Early the next morning, when Elisha's servant looked over the city wall and saw all those horses and chariots, he was frightened. Running to Elisha, he cried, "Oh, my lord, what shall we do?"

But Elisha wasn't troubled in the least. His trust in God was so great that nothing ever bothered him. "Don't be afraid," he said to the frightened young man. "Those who are with us are more than those who are with them."

The young man stared at him. How could this be? There was nobody in Dothan ready to fight these Arameans. Did Elisha have some secret army?

He did. And now he prayed, saying, "O Lord, open his eyes so he may see."

God answered the prayer. A moment later the young man

90

saw what Elisha had been looking at all the time. "Look!" he cried excitedly. "Look at them all!"

"He looked and saw the hills full of horses and chariots of fire all around Elisha." Elisha had seen those chariots of fire before, and he knew God was very near. "As the enemy came down toward him, Elisha prayed to the Lord, 'Strike these people with blindness.' "

It was a strange request, but he had a wonderful plan in mind. After God did as Elisha had asked, Elisha walked out of the city gate and bravely approached the leaders of the Aramean army. The men were milling about in their blindness, not knowing where they were or what to do.

" 'This is not the road,' he said to them, 'and this is not the city. Follow me, and I will lead you to the man you are looking for.' And he led them to Samaria"—right into Israel's capital.

When he had them all safely inside the city gates, he prayed, "Lord, open the eyes of these men so they can see." God did, and the soldiers saw with sudden fear that

they were in the middle of Samaria.

The king of Israel was delighted. Here was a splendid chance to teach the Arameans a lesson they would never forget. "Shall I kill them, my father? Shall I kill them?" he said to Elisha with relish.

"No, indeed!" said Elisha. Instead, he told the king to give the prisoners food and water, and then set them free to go back to their homes. "So he prepared a great feast for them, and after they had finished eating and drinking, he sent them away, and they returned to their master."

What a gracious, kindly deed that was! It was loving one's enemies in a very unusual way. And it worked, for a while at least. We read that "the bands from Aram stopped raiding Israel's territory."

It pays to have the protection of Elisha's secret army. You and I may have it, too. The Bible says, "The angel of the Lord encamps around those who fear him, and he delivers them." *

---

* Psalm 34:7.

Four Surprised Lepers

(2 Kings 6:24-7:20)

HOW MANY months passed before the Arameans forgot Elisha's great kindness to their soldiers, the Bible does not say. But they did forget, because the next thing we know is that Ben-Hadad, king of Aram, marched to Samaria and surrounded it.

This time, he told himself, there would be no mistake. The Arameans would finish off Israel once and for all. So they blocked every exit and sat outside waiting for the Israelites to starve to death.

As weeks and months went by, the stocks of food in Samaria grew lower and lower. Prices went up and up until "a donkey's head sold for eighty shekels of silver"—an enormous price. Only the rich could buy food. Some parents even cooked and ate their own children. The rest starved.

Never had there been such a famine. It was even worse than the drought in the days of Elijah, when there was no rain for three and a half years. Elisha was living in Samaria then, and he suffered along with the people. He knew that all this distress

93

had come as a result of the king's evil deeds, but the king blamed *him*.

At last, when things had become about as bad as they could get, the king vowed that he would kill Elisha that very day. An executioner was sent to carry out his threat, and the king followed to make sure his command was obeyed.

"Bar the door!" Elisha ordered when he learned of the plot against his life.

Soon there was a loud knocking, but he refused to open his door. Then he heard the voice of the king himself. He was saying, "This disaster is from the Lord. Why should I wait for the Lord any longer?"

Elisha called to him, "Hear the word of the Lord. . . . About this time tomorrow, a seah [10 pounds, or 4.5 kilograms] of flour will sell for a shekel [half ounce, or 14 grams] and two seahs of barley for a shekel at the gate of Samaria."

"Bah! The man must be mad!" exclaimed one of the men who had come with the king. "Even if the Lord should open the floodgates of the heavens, could this happen?"

The prices Elisha had quoted were so low that they must have seemed ridiculous compared with the famine prices they all were used to in the city. But though the man scoffed at him, Elisha didn't change his prophecy. Instead he said to him, "You will see it with your own eyes, . . . but you will not eat any of it!"

The king and his men went away. Perhaps the king said, "We'll give him one more day, and then if nothing happens, I will surely have him put to death."

94

As usual, Elisha wasn't troubled by these angry threats. He knew that the Arameans were about to leave. His secret army—the chariots of the Lord and all His shining angels—were about to move into action once more, and there was nothing to fear.

That very evening, in His own wonderful way, the Lord "caused the Arameans to hear the sound of chariots and horses and a great army, so that they said to one another, 'Look, the king of Israel has hired the Hittite and Egyptian kings to attack us!' So they got up and fled in the dusk and abandoned their tents and their horses and donkeys. They left the camp as it was and ran for their lives."

The first to discover that the Aramean army had gone were four lepers who had been slowly dying of hunger outside the gate of Samaria. As they sat talking by the gate that day, they said to one another, "We're going to die anyway. Let's go to the

Arameans and see if they will give us something to eat."

So as twilight fell they walked over to the Aramean camp and found nobody there. They couldn't believe their eyes. They thought there must be some mistake.

Going from tent to tent, they found the Arameans had left all their valuables behind—money, clothes, all sorts of things, and best of all, food! Heaps and piles of food! What a find! And what a feed! They stuffed themselves with the best of everything. Then they gathered up silver and gold and clothes of all kinds, and hid them.

After a while their consciences began to trouble them. They felt a bit selfish enjoying themselves while many people were starving to death inside the city. So they made their way back to the city gate after dark. They called the sleepy gatekeeper and told him their amazing story. He called the other gatekeepers, and though it was late at night, they sent word to the king.

He was in bed asleep when the news reached him. When his servants woke him up and told him the news, he didn't know whether to believe it or not. He was sure that even if it was true, it was only a trap the Arameans had set. They were probably waiting in the mountains for the Israelites to come

out, and then they would pounce upon them.

Somebody suggested that five horsemen be sent out to look things over. This seemed like a good idea, but they couldn't find five horses able to go. So they sent two.

These scouts followed the trail of the Arameans clear to the Jordan. All the way they found "clothing and equipment the Arameans had thrown away in their headlong flight."

When they got back to Samaria, word spread like wildfire about the empty camp. Soon the poor, starving people were pouring out of the city gates in thousands. They found so much food that there was enough to stock the shops again. Prices dropped so low that a seah of fine flour sold for a shekel and two seahs of barley sold for a shekel, just as Elisha had said.

As for the man who had laughed at Elisha's prophecy, the king put him in charge of the city gate to take care of the heavy traffic. But the crush was so great that he was knocked down, trampled on, and killed. He saw the cheap food—everybody was carrying some of it—but he never had a chance to eat any himself. It never pays to make fun of a prophet of the Lord.

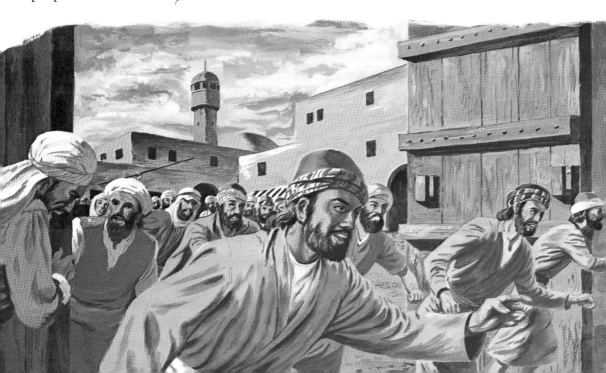

Making Iron Float

(2 Kings 4:38-44; 6:1-7)

GOD PERFORMED many miracles through His faithful servant Elisha. Perhaps it was because the times were so dark and His people were so poor and needy, that He revealed His power in so many wonderful ways.

Once when Elisha was visiting the group of prophets at Gilgal, he found that they had very little to eat. Seeing how hungry the young men were, he said, "Put on the large pot." Everybody began to look forward to a good meal.

While the food was cooking, one of the young men, anxious to help, brought a heap of wild gourds and cut them up into the pot, not knowing that they were poisonous.

When mealtime came, the young people sat around licking their lips. With Elisha in charge, they knew the meal would be good. Eagerly they watched as the food was poured from the pot.

Then came a bitter disappointment. Somebody recognized the taste of the wild gourds. "Don't eat!" he cried. "There is death in the pot."

Poor, hungry students! They all looked at Elisha, shocked that he had let them down like this. But he hadn't, and he wasn't even upset about the poisoned meal.

He asked for flour, and they brought some. Elisha stirred it into the pot. "Now start serving again," he said.

They did, and to their surprise, the bitter taste had gone and the poison had vanished.

Another time when he was meeting with a group of people—about 100 altogether—somebody brought him 20 loaves of barley bread and some heads of grain in a sack.

"Give it to the people to eat," he said.

"How can I set this before a hundred men?" his servant asked.

"Go ahead," said Elisha. "Give it to the people to eat. For this is what the Lord says: 'They will eat and have some left over.' "

It was just like Jesus' miracle of the loaves and fish more than 800 years later. There was plenty for everyone and lots left over.

One day the leaders of one of the companies of the prophets came to Elisha and reported that their buildings were overcrowded. There was no room for all the young people who wanted to attend. Would it be all right to put up a new building? They would cut the trees and do the rest of the work themselves to keep expenses down.

Elisha said the plan sounded good to him, and he wished them well.

"Come with us," they urged, anxious for his good advice.

100

"I will," he said, and went with them.

Arriving at the Jordan, they all began cutting down trees along the riverbank.

Suddenly there was a cry of alarm.

"My ax!" cried one of the young men. "The head has fallen off in the water! Oh, master, what shall I do? It was borrowed!"

"Where did it fall?" asked Elisha.

"Over there," said the young man, pointing to the place where it had disappeared.

Elisha cut a stick and threw it toward the spot, while everybody looked to see what would happen. Suddenly the axhead floated to the surface as though it had been made of wood.

"Pick it up," said Elisha as he walked away.

The young man did, his heart bursting with gratitude to his master and his God. 🌿

Arrows of Deliverance

(2 Kings 13:14-20)

GRADUALLY the years slipped by. Elisha moved from palaces to hovels, talking freely with kings and common people. Some loved him, others hated him. In a time of war, famine, and suffering, he was like a tower of strength to all who remained loyal to the God of heaven.

Then he fell sick with "the illness from which he died." While he was on his deathbed, Jehoash, king of Israel, came to visit him. With tears the king cried, "My father! My father! . . . The chariots and horsemen of Israel!" It was his way of saying how much the old prophet meant to him and his kingdom. And his words meant still more in view of the fact that he had just lost all but 10 of his chariots to the king of Aram.

Elisha knew how discouraged the king was, so he said, "Get a bow and some arrows."

The king did.

"Take the bow in your hands," said the old man.

The king obeyed, and Elisha put his hands upon the king's hands, to let him know that God would be with him.

102

"Open the east window," said Elisha.

Again the king did as he was asked.

"Shoot!" said Elisha. And he shot.

"The Lord's arrow of victory," cried the prophet as the feathered shaft sped toward the rising sun; "the arrow of victory over Aram! . . . You will completely destroy the Arameans at Aphek."

Then he said to the king, "Take the arrows."

The king took them.

"Strike the ground," said Elisha.

The king banged the arrows on the ground three times.

"No!" cried the prophet heatedly. "You should have struck the ground five or six times; then you would have defeated Aram and completely destroyed it."

Even the striking of the arrows on the ground meant more than the king understood. He should have banged those arrows down five, six, seven, ten times, to show his eagerness to do the work God wanted him to do.

After this Elisha became weaker and weaker, and he knew his end was near. Perhaps he wondered sometimes whether the fiery chariot that had taken Elijah to heaven would come for him. But no chariot came. So he died as others die, "and was buried."

Someday, however, in the glorious morning of the resurrection, he will awake to see that chariot after all, coming straight toward him, with the shining horsemen of heaven eager to carry him home.

PART THREE

Stories of
Conflict *and* Blessing

(2 Kings 13:21-16:20; 2 Chronicles 17:1-31:21)

The Choir That Won a Battle

(2 Chronicles 20:1-26)

A CHOIR doesn't often lead an army into battle, but that is what happened when Jehoshaphat was the king of Judah.

One day a messenger arrived in Jerusalem with news that the Moabites and Ammonites were on their way with thousands of soldiers to attack the city. Knowing the weakness of his own forces, Jehoshaphat turned to God for help. He also sent word to all the cities of Judah urging the people to come to the Temple and pray.

Soon fathers and mothers, boys and girls, began streaming into the city from all directions, packing the court of the house of the Lord. It must have been a marvelous sight. So many people were there that it seemed as though "all Judah" was standing humbly before the Lord "with their wives and children and little ones."

Good king Jehoshaphat began to pray a beautiful prayer. "O Lord, God of our fathers," he cried, "are you not the God who is in heaven? You rule over all the kingdoms of the nations.

107

← PAINTING BY PAUL REMMEY

As the enemy came near, the Lord gave Jahaziel a message for the people, "Be not afraid nor dismayed by reason of this great multitude; for the battle is not your's, but God's."

Power and might are in your hand, and no one can withstand you.

"O our God, did you not drive out the inhabitants of this land before your people Israel and give it forever to the descendants of Abraham your friend?"

He went on to remind God of Solomon's prayer at the dedication of the Temple: "If calamity comes upon us, whether the sword of judgment, or plague or famine, we will stand in your presence . . . and will cry out to you in our distress, and you will hear us and save us."

Then he told of the approach of the Moabites and the Ammonites, saying, "O our God, will *you* not judge them? For *we* have no power to face this vast army that is attacking us. We do not know what to do, but our eyes are upon you."

Scarcely had the king ended his prayer when the people heard another voice. Everyone turned to see who was speaking. It was young Jahaziel, a Levite, and it was clear that God had given him a message to cheer the people in this dark hour.

"This is what the Lord says to you:" he cried aloud, so that the whole great congregation could hear him. " 'Do not be afraid or discouraged because of this vast army. For the battle is not yours, but God's.' "

What a sigh of relief went up! God was going to help them! He had taken over the problem and was going to solve it in His own way!

THE CHOIR THAT WON A BATTLE

"You will not have to fight this battle," the young Levite continued. "Take up your positions; stand firm and see the deliverance the Lord will give you. . . . Do not be afraid; do not be discouraged. Go out to face them tomorrow, and the Lord will be with you."

As Jahaziel finished speaking king and people bowed humbly before God, thanking Him for His gracious promise of deliverance.

Nobody doubted that God would do as His prophet had said. Boldly Jehoshaphat declared, "Have faith in the Lord your God and you will be upheld; have faith in his prophets and you will be successful."

Early the next morning there was much bustle and excitement as the troops prepared to leave. Jehoshaphat moved among them speaking words of encouragement. As he was passing by, somebody had a bright idea. If God was going to win a great victory this day, why not thank Him for it in advance? Why not let the Temple choir go ahead and lead the whole army in songs of praise?

The king thought this was a fine suggestion. At once he "appointed men to sing to the Lord and to praise him for the splendor of his holiness." For the first time in history a choir went out to battle ahead of the soldiers. No doubt all the rest joined in, singing as they marched, "Give thanks to the Lord, for his love endures forever," their voices echoing back from the mountains.

What a scene to remember! Everyone who looked down from the city walls on that long column of singing men surely must have felt that this was one of the greatest moments in Jerusalem's history.

And what happened? The Bible says that "As they began to sing and praise, the Lord set ambushes against the men of Ammon and Moab and Mount Seir who were invading Judah, and they were defeated."

Exactly what took place we do not know, but it seems that suddenly the enemy soldiers began to quarrel among themselves. In the fighting that followed, thousands were killed, and when Jehoshaphat's singing army arrived on the scene, they found only dead bodies. They didn't have to fight at all, just as God had said through Jahaziel.

For three days they walked among the dead, gathering the things they could use—"a great amount of equipment and clothing and also articles of value—more than they could take away. There was so much plunder that it took three days to collect it. On the fourth day they assembled in the Valley of Beracah [or praise], where they praised the Lord. This is why it is called the Valley of Beracah to this day."

Jehoshaphat's army sang their way to victory. And because they trusted God, the valley of fear became the valley of blessing. 🖋

Baby Hid in the Temple

(2 Kings 8:16-18; 24-27; 11:1-21; 2 Chronicles 21:1-29:1)

WHEN good king Jehoshaphat died, much trouble came to the kingdom of Judah, just as it had come already to the northern kingdom of Israel. Jehoram, the new king, was very different from his father. He had married Athaliah, a daughter of the wicked king Ahab, and she had turned his heart from God to Baal.

The first thing he did when he took the throne was to kill all his brothers. What a dreadful thing to do! Then he went on to walk "in the ways of the kings of Israel."

Because of his sins God left him to face his enemies alone. When the Philistines and the Arabs came up to attack Jerusalem, no divine ambushes were set against them, and no chariots of fire came to the rescue. Instead, the enemy soldiers broke into the city, raided the king's palace, and took captive his wives and all his sons "except Ahaziah, the youngest." Soon after that Jehoram himself died of a very painful disease. He had reigned for eight years.

Ahaziah took his father's place on the throne and reigned

only one year. His mother Athaliah "encouraged him in doing wrong. He did evil in the eyes of the Lord, as the house of Ahab had done." When his uncle, the king of Israel, asked him to go to war against the Arameans, he did, only to be killed in the fighting.

Now a strange and terrible thing happened. When news of her son's death reached Athaliah, she set out to kill all his children—her own grandchildren!—thinking that if there was nobody else to take the throne, she would be queen.

She almost succeeded in her wicked scheme, but the children's aunt, Jehosheba, managed to save one of the children. When she heard how her nephews and nieces were being killed, this good woman grabbed little 1-year-old Joash and rushed him to the Temple buildings.

Being the high priest's wife, she knew the place well. She put the boy and his nurse in an out-of-the-way bedroom and locked them in. She guessed that nobody would think to search there, and nobody did.

Little Joash, like Samuel years before, grew up in the Temple. He lived there for nearly six years and was trained in

the ways of truth and right by his aunt and uncle.

Meanwhile thinking that everyone in the royal family was dead, the wicked Athaliah ruled as she pleased. She tried to get the people of Jerusalem to worship Baal as the Israelites in Samaria did.

Fortunately, Jehoiada the high priest was a true servant of the God of heaven. He hated all the evil the queen was doing. And he knew, better than anyone else, that she had no right to the throne. Quietly he gathered his friends around him, secretly telling them that the true heir was still alive.

I doubt whether he told anybody just where the boy was hidden, in case the queen heard about the secret. But he told enough so that no one doubted the truth of his words.

Gradually the spirit of revolt spread. As years passed, more and more people made up their minds to get rid of the usurper and put the rightful king on the throne.

At last the plot was ready. Jehoiada called the leading conspirators to meet him in the Temple. When everyone was present, he brought out little Joash, now 7 years old, for them to see. How they cheered and cheered! Jehoiada put a crown on the boy's head, while everybody shouted, "Long live the king! Long live the king!"

Hearing the noise, Queen Athaliah hurried over to the Temple to find out what it was all about. To her amazement, the place was filled with people singing and shouting for joy, led by trumpeters and the Temple choir.

Suddenly she caught sight of the little boy king, wearing a crown and royal robes. Who could this be? she wondered. She was sure she had killed all her grandsons—everybody who might have had a claim to the throne.

"Treason! Treason!" she screamed.

But no one came to help her. Instead, some of Jehoiada's men carried her out of the Temple and put her to death.

With the wicked usurper out of the way, a great procession was formed, and young King Joash was led in triumph to the king's house and placed upon the royal throne.

He must have looked very small and frightened in that big chair, but everybody was glad to see him there. "All the people of the land rejoiced. And the city was quiet" again. 🖋

Boy With a Money Box

(2 Kings 12:4-14; 2 Chronicles 24:4-14)

HAVING been brought up in the Temple by Jehoiada and his good wife Jehosheba, Joash chose to serve the God of heaven. So it was not surprising that he should want to repair the Temple, where he had spent most of his boyhood years.

He had many reasons for being thankful to God and to the priests who had watched over him so long at great risk to their lives. And Jehoiada had probably suggested to him more than once that he might show his gratitude by restoring the house of God.

It surely needed repair. Though less than 200 years had passed since its dedication, it was a wreck compared with what it had been in King Solomon's day. Not only had it been raided by the soldiers of Pharaoh Shishak and the Philistines and Arabs, but the sons of Queen Athaliah had "broken into the temple of God" and taken all the "sacred objects" and put them in the temple of Baal.

Soon after he was made king, Joash called the priests and

Levites together and ordered them to go to all the cities of Judah and gather money to repair the Temple. "And be quick about it," he told them, anxious that the work should be started as soon as possible.

The Levites, however, did not hurry themselves. Perhaps they said to one another, "The king is still a boy, so why should we take any notice of him?"

When the king learned that his command had been disobeyed and that money was only trickling in, he sent for Jehoiada and asked him what was the matter with the Levites and why they were so indifferent about their duties.

He wanted more speed, more action. Then, just like a boy, he suggested a very simple way to get the money quickly. What about putting a big box, or chest, outside the Temple gate and asking everybody to put something in it?

Jehoiada agreed that the idea was worth trying, and so, "at the king's command, a chest was made and placed outside, at the gate of the temple of the Lord."

The Bible doesn't say so, but I feel sure that King Joash was the first to put an offering into that chest, as a worthy example to his people. Right after him came the officials of the realm and all the merchants of the city, each dropping in some gift. As word about the king's money box spread through the country, people came flocking to Jerusalem by the thousands to see it. This was something new and different, and it was the boy king's own idea.

BOY WITH A MONEY BOX

Soon a long line of men and women, boys and girls, was waiting to put something in the box. Every moment some gold or silver was dropped into the chest and clinked as it hit the rest of the money inside. The children loved it.

Soon a servant ran to the king with news that the chest was full. It wouldn't hold another shekel. Joash could hardly believe his ears. He ordered that the chest be opened.

As "the royal secretary and the officer of the chief priest" opened up the chest before the king's officials and poured out piles of gold and silver, everyone was delighted. Probably most of them had never seen so much money before, for the priests of the Lord had been very poor during the reign of Queen Athaliah.

"Let it be filled again!" the king said, and the empty chest was put in its place outside the Temple, where more people were eagerly waiting to put money into it.

Soon the chest was full once more. Again it was emptied. The king was overjoyed at the success of his plan. "They did this regularly and collected a great amount of money."

As the silver and gold came in, it was used to hire "masons and carpenters . . . , and also workers in iron and bronze to repair the Temple."

How long it took to make all the repairs we are not told, but at last the work was done. When all the bills were paid, plenty of money was left over. This was used to make gold and silver containers for the priests to use in the Temple services.

Nobody knows what happened to the money box, but it served its purpose; and its story lets us see how even a little boy can have a very bright idea. ✐

The King Who Became a Leper

(2 Chronicles 24:15-26:21)

UNFORTUNATELY, the boy with the money box did not keep true to God all his life. It doesn't seem possible, but after the death of the high priest Jehoiada (at 130 years of age) some of the officials persuaded Joash to begin worshiping idols. Worse still, when Jehoiada's son Zechariah told him how wrong this was, Joash killed him.

After all the kindness Jehoiada had shown him, this was the meanest thing the king could have done. God was very displeased with him.

Punishment soon came. A band of Arameans attacked Jerusalem, sacked the city, killed the leaders, and left Joash himself badly wounded. Seeing him helpless in bed, two of his servants murdered him in revenge for Zechariah's murder. What a sad end for a boy who started well but lost his way and followed the advice of wicked men.

Amaziah took his place on the throne. He too started out well, and God gave him victories over his enemies. But he brought back idols from his defeated enemies and worshiped

119

them! A prophet of the Lord said to him, "Why do you consult this people's gods, which could not save their own people from your hand?"

Because of Amaziah's foolish deed God allowed trouble to happen to him. The king of Israel came from the north, broke down a large part of the wall of Jerusalem, and took away all the gold and silver out of the Temple.

All the money the people had so gladly dropped into Joash's money chest some years before was lost. What a pity! What a price there is to pay for sin!

The end of Amaziah was sad, too. His people revolted against him, chased him as far as Lachish, and killed him. Then they brought his body on horseback to Jerusalem for burial.

Taking Amaziah's place on the throne was a fine young man of 16, named Uzziah. His mother, Jecoliah, was a very good woman who had brought him up to love God. So "He did what was right in the eyes of the Lord."

Uzziah's reign was one of the longest in Judah's history—52 years—and "As long as he sought the Lord, God gave him success." And how God made Uzziah prosper! He subdued the Philistines and won victories over many other nations, extending his power to the border of Egypt.

He built up his army until he had more than 300,000 men armed with the very latest weapons, including machines "to shoot arrows and hurl large stones." He fortified Jerusalem by building new towers on the walls. "He also built towers . . . in

120

the foothills and in the plain" to protect his cisterns, vineyards, and cattle against his enemies.

The Bible says that "he was greatly helped until he became powerful." Then a real change came into his life. "After Uzziah became powerful, his pride led to his downfall."

All of us face the same danger. When we receive great blessings from God, we often think we won them by our own efforts! And the moment we do, we ask for trouble, for "pride goes before destruction." *

Because of all the success God had given him, Uzziah thought he could go into the Temple and burn incense like the priests. Why not? They weren't any better than he was.

When the high priest heard what the king had done, he followed him into the Temple, with 80 priests behind him. Uzziah was standing by the altar of incense, swinging a censer.

Boldly the high priest said to the king, "It is not right for you, Uzziah, to burn incense to the Lord. That is for the priests, the descendants of Aaron, who have been consecrated to burn incense. Leave the sanctuary, for you have been unfaithful; and you will not be honored by the Lord God."

At this the king lost his temper. How dare anyone question his right to go where he pleased in his kingdom—even into the Temple itself? Was the high priest more holy than he was? But as he stormed at the priests, a white spot appeared on his forehead. The priests recognized it at once, and a gasp of horror rose from them.

"Leprosy! Leprosy!" they cried.

When the king realized the awful truth of what had happened to him, he hurried out of the Temple, and the priests followed. He knew the disease was a judgment from God, and his pride quickly faded away.

King Uzziah was a leper the rest of his life. He had to live alone in a separate house, and he was never permitted to enter the Temple again.

He could have been "greatly helped" his whole life. His latter years could have been just as prosperous as his earlier years when he depended on God. What a pity he made that one mistake and let foolish pride spoil everything! ✎

---

* Proverbs 16:18.

Captives Set Free

(2 Kings 15:38-16:4; 2 Chronicles 27:1; 9-28:15)

JOTHAM, son of good king Uzziah, came to the throne
and reigned 16 years. He was followed by Ahaz, a very
wicked man, who not only made images of Baal but
"gathered together the furnishings from the temple of God
and took them away," shut the Temple doors, "and set up
altars at every street corner in Jerusalem." Worse still, he
even "sacrificed his sons in the fire, following the detestable
ways of the nations."

He was punished because of his dreadful sins. Soon he lost
all that his grandfather Uzziah had built up in the days when
God prospered him.

Judah was invaded by the Arameans, Edomites, and Philistines, who carried away many captives and stolen goods. The
Israelites swept through the land and took a large number of
prisoners. The Bible says, "The Israelites took captive from
their kinsmen two hundred thousand wives, sons and daughters." "They also took a great deal of plunder . . . back to
Samaria."

Imagine it! What a scene of misery! The wounded men, the frightened women, the sobbing boys and girls. What moans of anguish! What prayers for help!

There must have been many broken homes and broken hearts in Judah after these many attacks. How poor, how wretched, everybody who was left must have felt!

The heart of God was touched by the tragic sight. This was too much. Punishment had gone far enough. Before the sad procession reached Samaria, He had already sent someone to deliver them.

"A prophet of the Lord named Oded was there"—"there" where help was needed most.

This brave man went out to meet the soldiers who were bringing the prisoners to Samaria. As he saw the long, long line of men, women, and children, many tied together with ropes, others with feet cut and bleeding, all weak and weary after their long, forced march from Judah, his eyes glowed with anger.

Sternly he rebuked the soldiers. "Because the Lord, the God of your fathers, was angry with Judah, he gave them into your hand. But you have slaughtered them in a rage that reaches to heaven. And now you intend to make the men and women of Judah and Jerusalem your slaves. But aren't you also guilty of sins against the Lord your God?"

Then he commanded that the prisoners be released. "Now listen to me!" he cried earnestly. "Send back your fellow countrymen you have taken as prisoners, for the Lord's fierce anger rests on you."

The procession stopped. Prisoners who heard the prophet's

124

words took new hope. Word spread down the line that God had sent help. Their prayers were about to be answered. Bowed heads were raised, and tears were dried. Many a boy and girl looked up and said, "I told you so, Mamma; I knew God wouldn't forget us."

Meanwhile the leaders of the soldiers argued back and forth. Some said, "Why should we listen to this fellow? We're not going to give up our prisoners. Think of the trouble it cost us to get them!"

Then four very noble men spoke up. Their names were Azariah, Berekiah, Jehizkiah, and Amasa, and they deserve to be remembered among the great men of history.

These four were among the thousands of people who had come hurrying out of Samaria to meet the returning soldiers. They did not like what they saw. They agreed with the prophet Oded, and went even further. Very firmly they said to the soldiers, "You must not bring those prisoners here, . . . or we will be guilty before the Lord. Do you intend to add to our sin and guilt? For our guilt is already great, and his fierce anger rests on Israel."

Ashamed of what they had done, the soldiers slunk away, leaving the captives and the plunder.

Then these four noble men, Azariah, Berekiah, Jehizkiah, and Amasa, did one of the finest things mentioned in the Bible. They took all the poor captives and with the plunder (made up largely of clothing, as well as money), "clothed all who were naked. They provided them with clothes and sandals, food and drink, and healing balm. All those who were weak they put on donkeys. So they took them back to their fellow countrymen at Jericho, the City of Palms."

What a different procession it must have been going the other way—going back home again! All fears were gone, all tears were dried, all eyes were bright with thankfulness and new hope! How the boys and girls must have shouted for joy as they hopped and skipped about on that glorious homeward journey!

And how pleased God must have been with that gracious deed of the four noble men! If only there had been more men like them in Israel, the kingdom might have stood forever.

Two Wonderful Weeks

(2 Chronicles 29)

DO YOU remember Jehoiada, the high priest who cared for little Joash in the Temple? And do you remember how he had a son named Zechariah, who was later killed by that very same Joash? Well, this Zechariah had a little girl called Abijah who grew up to be one of the most important women in the Bible.

You see, Abijah, who loved the Lord, became the wife of King Ahaz. She had a son whom she called Hezekiah. While her wicked husband was trying to make the people of Judah turn to Baal, she was quietly bringing up her precious baby to love and honor the God of heaven.

What Abijah had to put up with we will never know, but through it all she kept true to the faith of her father and grandfather. And when Ahaz died, she had a son ready to sit on the throne who hated all the evil that his father had done.

Hezekiah was 25 years old when he began to reign. And thanks to his mother's careful training, "he did what was right in the eyes of the Lord."

TWO WONDERFUL WEEKS

His very first act after his coronation was to open the doors of the Temple which his father had closed. Then he ordered the Levites to go in and clean out all the dirt that had gathered while the place had been shut, and start the services again.

Before the work began, he called the priests and Levites together "in the square on the east side" and talked with them. After telling them to sanctify *themselves* before starting to cleanse the *Temple*, he went on to say, "Our fathers . . . did evil in the eyes of the Lord our God. . . .

"They also shut the doors of the portico and put out the lamps. They did not burn incense or present any burnt offerings. . . .

"Therefore, the anger of the Lord has fallen on Judah and Jerusalem; he has made them an object of dread and horror and scorn, as you can see with your own eyes. This is why our fathers have fallen by the sword and why our sons and daughters and our wives are in captivity.

"Now I intend to make a covenant with the Lord, the God of Israel, so that his fierce anger will turn away from us.

"My sons, do not be negligent now, for the Lord has chosen you to stand before him and serve him."

Encouraged by the king, everybody went to work with a will. And how they put their hearts into the job!

"The priests went into the sanctuary of the Lord to purify it. They brought out to the courtyard of the Lord's temple everything unclean that they found in the temple of the Lord." The Levites carried the rubbish out of the city

— PAINTING BY HERBERT RUDEEN

Due to his good mother's careful training, the first act of the young King Hezekiah after his coronation was to open the doors of the Temple which his father years before had closed.

and dumped it into the Kidron Valley.

It took a whole week to get the worst of the job done, and another week to finish it properly. Then both priests and Levites went to King Hezekiah to report. "We have purified the entire temple of the Lord, the altar of burnt offering with all its utensils, and the table for setting out the consecrated bread . . . ," they said. "We have prepared and consecrated all the articles that King Ahaz removed in his unfaithfulness while he was king. They are now in front of the Lord's altar."

Hezekiah was surprised that they had finished so soon, and he was very, very pleased. The next morning he rose early, and taking all the rulers of the city with him, went to the Temple. As a sacrifice he brought seven bulls, seven rams, seven male lambs, seven male goats, and he "commanded the priests, the descendants of Aaron, to offer these on the altar of the Lord." This was a sin offering for all Israel.

As soon as the fire was lit and the smoke of the sacrifice began to rise into the early morning air, there was a burst of

130

song and music. Priests blew the sacred trumpets while Levites played on cymbals, lyres, and harps and sang to the Lord.

Everybody was happy that the Temple was open again and that from now on the worship of God would continue as it had years before. "The whole assembly bowed in worship, while the singers sang and the trumpeters played."

It was a great day. After the sin offering had been completed, Hezekiah asked the people to bring thank offerings, which they did with cheerful hearts. Six hundred bulls and 3,000 sheep were brought—so many that there weren't enough priests to handle them, and "their kinsmen the Levites" had to help them.

It must have been a wonderful sight with so many people eagerly bringing their gifts. Jerusalem hadn't seen anything like this for a long time. "Hezekiah and all the people rejoiced at what God had brought about for his

people, because it was done so quickly."

"Quickly" was the word. Little more than two weeks had passed since the doors of the Temple had been unlocked and the work of cleaning up begun.

Some people had thought it might take months, maybe years, before the place could be fixed up properly so the worship of God could be started again. But it had happened in just two weeks—two wonderful weeks!

It seemed too good to be true. But it was true! The Temple was open. Worship had begun. The smoke of the sacrifices was billowing heavenward. No wonder Hezekiah was happy! So was his mother, Abijah. For her, it was a dream come true. This was her moment of triumph after all the dark years she had lived with wicked Ahaz. How her father and her grandfather would have rejoiced to see this day!

It just goes to show how quickly a task can be done when people *want* to do it. It doesn't have to wait and wait and wait. When there are willing hearts, and a desire to serve, the thing can be done quickly.

Great Joy in Jerusalem

(2 Chronicles 30)

CHEERED by what happened when the Temple was opened again, King Hezekiah suggested to his counselors that it would be a fine thing if the whole nation—Israel as well as Judah—could celebrate the Passover together as they had done years before.

It was a bold idea, for only a few years had passed since soldiers from Samaria had taken away those 200,000 captives we read about. Imagine proposing to throw open the gates of Jerusalem to people who could be so cruel!

But the king was so sure he was right and that God would bless the plan that he persuaded everybody to agree to it. Then he sent messengers all over Palestine, "from Beersheba to Dan," inviting the people "to come to Jerusalem and celebrate the Passover to the Lord, the God of Israel."

The messengers carried letters from the king and his officials throughout all Israel and Judah. "People of Israel," the letters began, "return to the Lord, the God of Abraham, Isaac and Israel, that he may return to you. . . . Submit to the Lord.

Come to the sanctuary. . . . Serve the Lord your God. . . . If you return to the Lord, then your brothers and your children will be shown compassion by their captors and will come back to this land, for the Lord your God is gracious and compassionate. He will not turn his face from you if you return to him."

It was a very beautiful message and much more important than anybody—even Hezekiah himself—understood at the moment. In fact, it was Israel's last chance, their last hope of escape from the doom that was so near.

Already the Assyrians had invaded northern Palestine and taken away many captives. Soon—very soon—the same enemy would return and carry off almost the whole population. If the people of Israel had accepted Hezekiah's invitation, and turned from their sins, God would have saved them as He saved Jerusalem. But they did not accept it.

As Hezekiah's messengers "went from town to town . . . , the people scorned and ridiculed them." Some thought it was a trick. Others said it was foolish trying to get so many people to travel to Jerusalem in such dangerous times. "What's the use?"

asked others. "Why revive the old Passover service now?"

A few accepted the invitation, but in general the response from Israel was not good.

In Judah, however, the people had "unity of mind to carry out what the king and his officials had ordered." They came to Jerusalem by thousands, and "a very large crowd of people assembled in Jerusalem to celebrate the Feast of Unleavened Bread."

When everybody arrived, the first thing they did was remove every trace of idol worship from Jerusalem. The people broke down all the altars that had been built in honor of heathen gods and threw them into the Kidron Valley.

Then the service of the Passover began. Because of the crowds, many of those who had come from a distance had not been able to wash themselves as they were supposed to do before taking part in this very solemn service. But when Hezekiah heard about it, he prayed to God for them. "May the Lord, who is good," he said, "pardon everyone who sets his heart on seeking God—the Lord, the God of his fathers—even if he is not clean according to the rules of the sanctuary.' "

That prayer showed what a great man Hezekiah was. He believed God cares more about what goes on inside a person's heart than how clean his hands or feet may be. And he was right. The Bible says "the Lord heard Hezekiah and healed the people."

What a glorious time they had together! For seven days

135

they kept the feast "with great rejoicing, while the Levites and priests sang to the Lord every day, accompanied by the Lord's instruments of praise." The people enjoyed themselves so much that they decided to keep the feast another seven days, and the second week was as happy as the first.

"The entire assembly of Judah rejoiced, along with . . . all who had assembled from Israel, including the aliens who had come from Israel and those who lived in Judah. There was great joy in Jerusalem, for since the days of Solomon son of David king of Israel there had been nothing like this in Jerusalem."

Heaps and Heaps of Blessings

(2 Chronicles 31)

FILLED with joy over the turn events had taken, the people streamed out of Jerusalem with their minds made up to put an end to idol worship once and for all. They went through all the cities of Judah breaking images to pieces and smashing altars until "they had destroyed all of them."

This done, Hezekiah suggested that the people start paying tithe (a tenth of their earnings) again for the support of the priests and Levites and the work of the house of God. The people gladly agreed. They were all so happy about the wonderful reformation taking place that as soon as they heard about the king's wishes, they began bringing gifts.

"The Israelites generously gave the firstfruits of their grain, new wine, oil and honey and all that the fields produced. They brought a great amount, a tithe of everything." They also "brought a tithe of their herds and flocks and a tithe of the holy things dedicated to the Lord their God, and they piled them in heaps."

HEAPS AND HEAPS OF BLESSINGS

Nothing like this had happened before—at least, not since the days of Solomon. The people brought so many offerings that the regular places of storage weren't big enough to hold them all. "They began doing this in the third month and finished in the seventh month." In other words, for four months people kept bringing their tithes and gifts until there were heaps and heaps and heaps, all over the place.

Hearing what had happened, the king went to see for himself. "When Hezekiah and his officials came and saw the heaps, they praised the Lord and blessed his people Israel."

The priests blessed the people too, for this was the first time in years that they had had enough to eat. "This great amount," Azariah the chief priest told the king, "is left over" after the priests and Levites had eaten all they wanted.

PAINTING BY HARRY ANDERSON

As for the dear people, they did not lose anything because they were so generous. No, indeed. While they gave heaps and heaps of their good things to God, He gave them heaps and heaps of blessings in return.

Now the question arose as to what should be done with all that the people had brought in. Hezekiah thought of a practical solution. He had storerooms built inside the Temple. This was done, and the Levites "faithfully brought in the contributions, tithes and dedicated gifts." There was so much that Hezekiah appointed a committee of 12 men to look after it, with Conaniah as chairman.

As the years passed, it seemed as if everything that King Hezekiah started was a success. This was because "in everything that he undertook in the service of God's temple and in obedience to the law and the commands, he sought his God and worked wholeheartedly. And so he prospered."

That sort of program will spell success for anybody.

PART FOUR

Stories of
Kings and Prophets

(2 Kings 17:1-25:30; 2 Chronicles 32:1-36:21;
Isaiah, Jeremiah, Lamentations)

Why Israel Fell

(*2 Kings 17:1-18*)

JUST a few short years after that wonderful Passover in Jerusalem, Samaria fell to the Assyrians, and the kingdom of Israel came to an end. Hoshea was on the throne at the time, the last of the kings of Israel. Like all who had reigned before him, "he did evil in the eyes of the Lord."

Shalmaneser, king of Assyria, had asked Hoshea for a very large sum of money. Unable to pay it, Hoshea had turned to King So of Egypt for help instead of to God. This was a big mistake, for not only was King So unable to help him, but when King Shalmaneser heard what Hoshea had done, he was furious.

Marching to Samaria with a huge army, he surrounded the city. The siege lasted three years, and many of the people inside died of starvation. This time there was no Elisha to come to the rescue and no chariots of the Lord to frighten away the invaders.

No doubt Hoshea and his people cried to Baal to save them, but no help came. It was the final proof to the people of

143

When Hoshea, king of Israel, turned to Baal instead of to the true God for help in the siege of Samaria, the Assyrians broke down the gates and drove all the people into captivity.

Israel that all the idols they had worshiped were worthless.

At last everybody was too feeble to resist any longer. The gates of the city were broken open, and the Assyrian soldiers rushed in. Many people were killed, and the rest were carried away into captivity.

The same thing happened in every city and village of Israel, for "the king of Assyria invaded the entire land." He "deported the Israelites to Assyria. He settled them in Halah, in Gozan on the Habor River and in the towns of the Medes."

It was a sad, sad ending to what could have been a glorious history. In little more than 200 years Israel had fallen from its place among the greatest and richest nations on earth to a scattered group of wretched, poverty-stricken captives.

In just 200 years they had lost everything—their land, their homes, their furniture, their cattle, their money, their honor. They had nothing left of all that God had given them.

And why? Because they had turned away from the God of heaven. From Jeroboam to Hoshea, just 20 kings sat on the throne of Israel, and every one of them was a rebel against God.

Every one of them worshiped Baal and led the people into evil.

"Samaria fell because the Israelites sinned against the Lord their God, who had rescued them from the king of Egypt. . . . They . . . followed the customs of the people whom the Lord had driven out as his people advanced. . . .

"The Israelites did things that the Lord their God disapproved of. . . .

"On all the hills and under every shady tree they put up stone pillars and images of the goddess Ashterah, and they burned incense on all the pagan altars, following the practice of the people whom the Lord had driven out of the land. They aroused the Lord's anger with all their wicked deeds and disobeyed the Lord's command not to worship idols" (TEV).

Time and again God had pleaded with them to turn from their wickedness. He had sent Elijah, Elisha, and other prophets to them saying, "Turn from your evil ways. Observe my commands and decrees." "But they would not listen and were as stiff-necked as their fathers, who did not trust in the Lord their God. . . .

"They forsook all the commands of the Lord their God and made for themselves two idols cast in the shape of calves, and an Asherah pole. They bowed down to all the starry hosts, and

they worshiped Baal.

"They sacrificed their sons and daughters in the fire. They practiced divination and sorcery and sold themselves to do evil in the eyes of the Lord, provoking him to anger.

"So the Lord was very angry with Israel and removed them from his presence."

If the people of Israel had remained true to God, they would have been wonderfully blessed. They would have enjoyed great honor and riches. They would have been protected from the Assyrians and all their enemies. They would have been respected by all nations for their goodness and sincerity. Their towns and villages would have been models of order, beauty, and prosperity for all the world to copy.

But in spite of everything God had done to encourage them in the right way and to warn them of what was evil, the people of Israel had insisted on ignoring God's advice. Now He could only leave them to the results of their own choices. Lashed by the whip of their conquerors, naked and barefoot, starving and frozen, the Israelites stumbled along the long hard trail to captivity.

What a price they had to pay for turning away from God!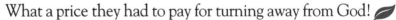

Youth With a Vision

(Isaiah)

A T THE very time that all these terrible things were happening to Israel, God raised up one of the greatest prophets who ever lived to speak words of warning and comfort to His people.

Just when Isaiah was born we are not told, but it must have been not very long after the death of Elisha. At least we know that he lived through the reigns of "Uzziah, Jotham, Ahaz and Hezekiah, kings of Judah." This means that he also lived through the reigns of the last seven kings of Israel, from Jeroboam II to Hoshea.

If we remember this, it will help us to understand many things that Isaiah wrote. How fitting were his words concerning Israel. "Ah, sinful nation, a people loaded with guilt, a brood of evildoers, children given to corruption! They have forsaken the Lord; they have spurned the Holy One of Israel and turned their backs on him. . . .

"Your country is desolate, your cities burned with fire; your fields are being stripped by foreigners right before

you, laid waste as when overthrown by strangers.

"The Daughter of Zion [Jerusalem] is left like a shelter in a vineyard, like a hut in a field of melons, like a city under siege."

Isaiah's call to the work of a prophet came at the end of the reign of Uzziah, before the people of Samaria were carried into captivity by the Assyrians. He tells us about it himself.

"In the year that King Uzziah died," he says, "I saw the Lord seated on a throne, high and exalted, and the train of his robe filled the temple."

Above the throne he saw seraphs, each with six wings. Two wings covered the face and two covered the feet of each wonderful creature, while the other two were used for flight.

"And they were calling to one another: 'Holy, holy, holy is the Lord Almighty; the whole earth is full of his glory.' " The doorposts trembled at the sound of the voice, and the building was filled with smoke.

"Woe to me!" cried the young man. "I am ruined! For I am a man of unclean lips, and I live among a people of unclean lips, and my eyes have seen the King, the Lord Almighty."

Suddenly one of the seraphs picked up "a live coal" from the altar of incense and flew with it to Isaiah. Lightly touching the young man's mouth with the burning ember he said, "See, this has touched your lips; your guilt is taken away and your sin atoned for."

149

← PAINTING BY RUSSELL HARLAN

Surrounded by the glory of heaven while worshiping in the Temple, Isaiah cried, "I am a man of unclean lips," and an angel touched his lips with a glowing coal off the altar.

Then through the smoke came another voice saying, "Whom shall I send? And who will go for us?"

It was the voice of God! The Lord Himself was calling him to service! Humbly Isaiah answered, "Here am I. Send me!"

"Go," said God, giving him the message he was to tell the people.

And so the prophet Isaiah began his lifework. "In the year that King Uzziah died," when everybody in Jerusalem was fearful and worried about the future, Isaiah saw the King Eternal, seated on the throne of the universe—the one throne that will never pass away.

This vision never left him. All through the reign of wicked King Ahaz, all through the terrible invasions of Israel and Judah by the kings of Assyria, he remembered what he had seen and heard that wonderful night. Others might give up hope, but not he. He knew for sure that God lives and reigns and must be victorious at last.

In the dark and evil times in which he lived, Isaiah talked courage and hope. Someday God would raise up a Deliverer. Someday God's people would rejoice and say, "To us a child is born, to us a son is given, and the government will be on his shoulders. And he will be called Wonderful Counselor, Mighty God, Everlasting Father, Prince of Peace. Of the increase of his government and peace there will be no end. He will reign on David's throne and over his kingdom, establishing and uphold-

ing it with justice and righteousness from that time on and forever."

How comforting this promise must have sounded in those days of war, invasion, suffering, and death! So that no one would doubt whether it would ever come true, he added, "The zeal of the Lord Almighty will accomplish this."

Again he said to the worried and sorrowing people, "Lift up your eyes to the heavens, look at the earth beneath; the heavens will vanish like smoke, the earth will wear out like a garment and its inhabitants die like flies. But my salvation will last forever, my righteousness will never fail."

To cheer their hearts still more he said, " 'Though the mountains be shaken and the hills be removed, yet my unfailing love for you will not be shaken nor my covenant of peace be

removed,' says the Lord, who has compassion on you."

"Seek the Lord while he may be found; call on him while he is near," he urged. "Let the wicked forsake his way and the evil man his thoughts. Let him turn to the Lord, and he will have mercy on him, and to our God, for he will freely pardon."

The time would come, he assured them, when all evil will come to an end.

"Give strength to hands that are tired and to knees that tremble with weakness. Tell everyone who is discouraged, 'Be strong and don't be afraid! God is coming to your rescue, coming to punish your enemies' " (TEV).

"Then will the eyes of the blind be opened and the ears of the deaf unstopped.

"Then will the lame leap like a deer, and the mute tongue shout for joy. . . .

"And the ransomed of the Lord will return. They will enter Zion with singing; everlasting joy will crown their heads. Gladness and joy will overtake them, and sorrow and sighing will flee away."

There will be no more war, no more suffering, no more death. People will build houses and plant gardens without fear of invaders, and "long enjoy the work of their hands." Then there will be peace and friendship all over the world. " 'They will neither harm nor destroy on all my holy mountain,' says the Lord."

That was the beautiful message God gave Isaiah, who when he was just a young man, saw God on His throne. ✐

153

Isaiah described his vision of the beautiful new earth, free from all fear and unhappiness, where Jesus will dwell with those who have been faithful to Him and obedient to His law.

Angel to the Rescue

(2 Kings 18:13-19:37; 2 Chronicles 32:1-22; Isaiah 36 and 37)

SOME years after the Assyrians had captured Samaria, they invaded Judah and tried to take Jerusalem. Sennacherib was king of Assyria now, and he came up, "attacked all the fortified cities of Judah and captured them."

Jerusalem alone was left. In all the country that God had given to the people He had brought out of Egypt, this was the only city they still owned. All the others, from Dan to Beersheba, had been lost.

Never had the City of David seemed so lonesome up on its mountaintop. Many must have wondered how it could possibly stand against Assyria's strength. No doubt some said, "If Jerusalem is taken, what hope will remain that the promises to Abraham, Isaac, and Jacob will ever be fulfilled? How will Eve's Offspring ever crush the snake's head?"

Fortunately, behind Jerusalem's barricaded gates, were two great men and one noble woman: Isaiah the prophet, Hezekiah the king, and Abijah, or "Abi," the king's mother. Anxious to avoid an attack if possible, Hezekiah sent messen-

154

gers to Sennacherib, asking if money would satisfy him. The invader set a stiff price: 11 tons (10 metric tons) of silver and one ton (not quite one metric ton) of gold.

Hezekiah tried to raise the money, even taking the gold overlay off the doors and pillars of the Temple. He sent everything he had been able to collect to Sennacherib, but the Assyrian king was not satisfied. He wanted more. He said he was going to take the city anyway, and Hezekiah might as well open the gates and surrender.

But Hezekiah was not the sort of man to give up without a fight. He talked the matter over with his officials, and they decided to resist. First they blocked up all the sources of water outside the city. "Why should the kings of Assyria come," they said, "and find plenty of water?"

Then they "worked hard repairing all the broken sections of the wall and building towers on it" and made weapons and shields.

Gathering all his military officers together, Hezekiah en-

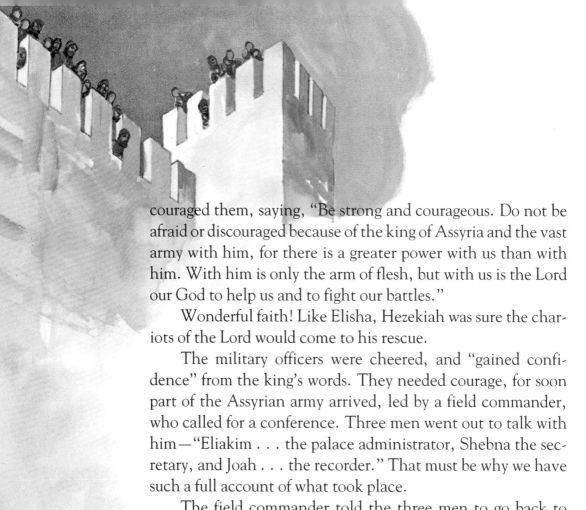

couraged them, saying, "Be strong and courageous. Do not be afraid or discouraged because of the king of Assyria and the vast army with him, for there is a greater power with us than with him. With him is only the arm of flesh, but with us is the Lord our God to help us and to fight our battles."

Wonderful faith! Like Elisha, Hezekiah was sure the chariots of the Lord would come to his rescue.

The military officers were cheered, and "gained confidence" from the king's words. They needed courage, for soon part of the Assyrian army arrived, led by a field commander, who called for a conference. Three men went out to talk with him—"Eliakim . . . the palace administrator, Shebna the secretary, and Joah . . . the recorder." That must be why we have such a full account of what took place.

The field commander told the three men to go back to King Hezekiah and tell him that there was no point in resisting

any longer. If he was looking for help from the Egyptians, he was leaning on a broken reed. If he was trusting in the God of heaven, he was equally mistaken, because the Lord had told the king of Assyria to come and destroy Jerusalem.

Eliakim, Shebna, and Joah begged him to talk in Aramaic, not Hebrew, so that the people listening on the city wall would not understand. But the field commander refused. Instead, he raised his voice and shouted, "Have any of the gods of the nations delivered their lands out of the hand of the king of Assyria? Where are the gods of Hamath and Arpad? Name the gods who have delivered their countries!"

There was no reply from the people on the walls, for King Hezekiah had told everybody, "Do not answer him." But when the council was over and the field commander had gone away, Hezekiah was very upset. He sent Eliakim, Shebna, and Joah to Isaiah to tell him all that had happened.

When they returned to the king, they brought this message from the Lord: "Do not be afraid. . . . I am going to put such a spirit in him that when he hears a certain report, he will return to his own country."

The field commander heard that his king was fighting somewhere else, so he left Jerusalem for the battlefront. But the threat to Jerusalem was not over. Eventually a letter arrived from the king of Assyria, repeating all that the field commander had said and demanding again that the city be surrendered. When Hezekiah read it, "he went up to the temple of the Lord and spread it out before the Lord." Then he prayed.

"O Lord, God of Israel," he cried, "enthroned between the cherubim, you alone are God over all the kingdoms of the earth. You have made heaven and earth.

"Give ear, O Lord, and hear; open your eyes, O Lord, and see; listen to the words Sennacherib has sent to insult the living God.

"It is true, O Lord, that the Assyrian kings have laid waste these nations and their lands. They have thrown their gods into the fire and destroyed them, for they were not gods but only wood and stone, fashioned by men's hands.

"Now, O Lord our God, deliver us from his hand, so that all kingdoms on earth may know that you alone, O Lord, are God."

What a beautiful prayer, so earnest, so full of faith and trust! God heard it, and He sent Isaiah immediately to tell Hezekiah not to worry any longer. "Therefore this is what the Lord says concerning the king of Assyria," Isaiah told Hezekiah. " 'He will not enter this city or shoot an arrow here.

158

He will not come before it with shield or build a siege ramp against it. By the way that he came he will return; he will not enter this city, declares the Lord.

" 'I will defend this city and save it, for my sake and for the sake of David my servant!' "

Wonderful promise! God Himself was going to defend the city. He knew exactly what was going to happen and how the enemy would be turned back. Everyone could relax.

That very night the angel of the Lord went into action, killing the Assyrian soldiers. Exactly how it happened the Bible does not say, but by morning, there were 185,000 dead soldiers lying all over the countryside around Jerusalem.

People crowded to the walls to see the amazing sight. They could hardly believe their eyes, for not an arrow had been shot or a stone thrown. Yet there were their enemies, dead! The Assyrian army had been destroyed!

As for the mighty Sennacherib, "he withdrew to his own land in disgrace," where two of his sons put him to death.

The Sun Turns Back

(2 Kings 20:1-11; Isaiah 38:1-8)

ONE OF the most wonderful events in history occurred during the reign of Hezekiah. The king had fallen sick, and Isaiah had told him that he was going to die.

But Hezekiah did not want to die. So he "turned his face to the wall and prayed to the Lord, 'Remember, O Lord, how I have walked before you faithfully and with wholehearted devotion and have done what is good in your eyes.' " As he prayed, he "wept bitterly."

God heard His faithful servant. Before Isaiah had gone as far as the middle court of the king's house, "the word of the Lord came to him: 'Go back and tell Hezekiah, the leader of my people, "This is what the Lord, the God of your father David, says: I have heard your prayer and seen your tears; I will heal you. On the third day from now you will go up to the temple of the Lord. I will add fifteen years to your life." ' "

No one knows how far it was from the king's bedroom to

160

the middle court, but God's answer came in the little time it took Isaiah to walk that distance. Hezekiah then asked if he could have a sign that the Lord was really going to heal him.

Yes, Isaiah said, he could. And he could choose one of two. Pointing to the stairway King Ahaz had built to tell the time, he asked if the king would like the shadow on the stairs to "go forward ten steps" or "go back ten steps."

Now, Hezekiah was a very sick man who had just been weeping heartbrokenly at the thought of approaching death. But his mind was still keen enough to see that if the shadow went *forward* ten steps, it wouldn't mean very much. That's the way the shadow usually moved as the day progressed. But if the shadow went *backward* ten steps—

JUSTINEN CREATIVE GROUP

well, that would be a very big miracle indeed.

"Have it go back ten steps," he asked. So Isaiah cried earnestly to God to do this marvelous thing. As the prophet prayed, the king watched the stairway from his bed. Surely it could not be! Yes! The shadow was moving. Not forward, but backward!

Nothing like this had ever happened before! It was beyond belief. But it was happening. Back, back, back it went. One step, two steps, three steps, four steps. Miracle of miracles! eight, nine, ten steps!

Hezekiah must have gasped in amazement. For a moment, perhaps, he thought he had asked too much. For here was God upsetting the whole universe—or so it seemed—to answer his simple and rather thoughtless prayer.

It just shows how much God is prepared to do for those who love and trust Him with all their hearts. At times He will even make the sun turn back in the sky, rather than disappoint one of His faithful children.

Visitors From Babylon

(2 Kings 20:12-17; Isaiah 39:1-6)

HOW DID the miracle of the sun's shadow on the stairway happen? Nobody knows. But it *must* have happened, because people watching the sun's shadow in Babylon hundreds of miles away also saw it go backward at exactly the same time. It must have been noticed all around the world. Everywhere people wondered what it meant.

As for Hezekiah, he got better, just as Isaiah had said. Within three days he was back at work, as healthy as ever. He wrote these words about his experience: "Surely it was for my benefit that I suffered such anguish. In your love you kept me from the pit of destruction; you have put all my sins behind your back.

"For the grave cannot praise you, death cannot sing your praise; those who go down to the pit cannot hope for your faithfulness.

"The living, the living—they praise you as I am doing today."

Some weeks later important visitors arrived in Jerusalem. They were ambassadors from Babylon with letters and a present from King Merodach-Baladan to congratulate Hezekiah on his recovery. They had also come "to ask him about the miraculous sign that had occurred in the land" * that everyone was talking about.

Hezekiah was delighted. It must have been very comforting to him just then to find that he had a few friends left. With Jerusalem the only city in all Palestine standing out against the power of the Assyrians, he must sometimes have felt very, very lonesome.

So he gave the Babylonian ambassadors a great welcome. Gladly he told them how the shadow had moved back on his stairway and how it had been a sign that he would recover from his illness and live another 15 years.

Then with no little pride he showed them his "storehouses—the silver, the gold, the spices and the fine oil— his armory and everything found among his treasures."

What the ambassadors thought of it all, we are not told. No doubt they made a mental note of everything Hezekiah had and where he stored it, in case this information might come in handy sometime. They knew their royal master, the Babylonian king, would certainly be interested to learn where a nice little store of gold and silver could be found.

At last the ambassadors said goodbye, with many kind words and good wishes from Hezekiah and the people of Jerusalem. Hardly had they disappeared down the hill, however, when Isaiah turned up at the royal palace. He wanted to know

all about the visitors and what they had said.

"Oh," said Hezekiah, still very happy at what had happened, "they came from Babylon."

"What did they see in your palace?" Isaiah asked next.

"Everything," said Hezekiah proudly, no doubt thinking Isaiah would be pleased with the courtesy he had shown his guests.

But the prophet was not pleased. Hezekiah had made a mistake. He should not have paraded his wealth before these strangers. "Hear the word of the Lord," Isaiah said. "The time will surely come when everything in your palace, and all that your fathers have stored up until this day, will be carried off to

Babylon. Nothing will be left, says the Lord."

The king was shocked. He had never thought of this. Of course, he should have been more careful, but now it was too late. Those men had seen everything, and they would tell their king about it. His best-kept secrets would be known not only in Babylon, but maybe in Nineveh, too. How foolish he had been!

We all should be careful in every word and action. One thoughtless deed, prompted by pride, can bring such unhappy consequences. How much wiser are those who show their visitors, not the treasures of their homes, but the riches of God's love toward them. 🖋

———————
* 2 Chronicles 32:31.

The Bad Boy King

(2 Kings 20:21-21:18; 2 Chronicles 32:33-33:16)

EXACTLY 15 years after the miracle of the sun's shadow that moved backward on the stairway, Hezekiah died. Taking his place on the throne was his young son, Manasseh, one of the worst kings Judah ever had.

How such a good father came to have such a bad son is a mystery. Whatever the cause, Manasseh was a little rebel from the start. He delighted in defying his father and going against his wishes. As soon as he came to the throne, he got right to work undoing all the good his father had done. He gave orders to rebuild the altars to the heathen gods that Hezekiah had destroyed. He brought back Baal worship to Jerusalem, and "bowed down to all the starry hosts and worshiped them."

His greatest sin was placing a carved image in the Temple itself—a shocking insult to the God of heaven, who had commanded His people, "You shall not make for yourself an idol in the form of anything in heaven above or on the earth beneath or in the waters below. You shall not bow down to them or worship them." *

Besides all this, Manasseh brought back all the wicked ways of the heathen. "He sacrificed his sons in the fire . . . , practiced sorcery, divination and witchcraft, and consulted mediums and spiritists. He did much evil in the eyes of the Lord, provoking him to anger."

Isaiah was dead by now, perhaps killed by Manasseh, who "shed so much innocent blood." But God sent other prophets to warn the young king what would happen to him if he continued in his evil course. Through one of them He said: "Manasseh king of Judah has committed these detestable sins. . . . Therefore this is what the Lord, the God of Israel, says: I am going to bring such disaster on Jerusalem and Judah that the ears of everyone who hears of it will tingle. . . . I will wipe out Jerusalem as one wipes a dish, wiping it and turning it upside down."

But though God spoke so plainly to Manasseh and his people, they would not listen. As a result, He allowed them to be conquered. The Assyrians came and took Manasseh captive. The carved image he had put in the Temple did not save him, nor did all the heathen gods he had worshiped. Bound with chains, he was carried to Babylon.

How long he remained in prison in a foreign land, we are not told, but while he was there, he remembered his kind father and his father's God. He came to see what a dreadful mistake he had made and asked God to forgive him.

"In his distress he sought the favor of the Lord his God and

humbled himself greatly before the God of his fathers. And when he prayed to him, the Lord was moved by his entreaty and listened to his plea."

Very wonderfully, God forgave him—even though he *had* put a carved image in the Temple. God "brought him back to Jerusalem and to his kingdom. Then Manasseh knew that the Lord is God."

Converted at last, Manasseh tried to make up for all the wrong he had done in his youth. First of all, he took that ugly idol out of the house of the Lord. Then he broke down all the altars he had built in Jerusalem and "threw them out of the city." He also "restored the altar of the Lord and sacrificed fellowship offerings and thank offerings on it, and told Judah to serve the Lord, the God of Israel."

So the bad boy king made good in the end. But what a pity he made such a mess of things at first! What wasted years! What needless suffering!

Manasseh's reign lasted 55 years. What a glorious reign it might have been had he always remained true to God and followed in his father's footsteps! ✒

---

* Exodus 20:4, 5.

The Good Boy King

(2 Kings 21:18-23:23; 2 Chronicles 33:20-35:19)

AFTER Manasseh died, his son Amon came to the throne. But he reigned only two years. A bad lad, as his father had been, he was killed by his officials. Then his little boy Josiah became king.

Josiah was only 8 years old at the time of his coronation, and that's very young to be a king. He must have had a very good mother, because from the start, "He did what was right in the eyes of the Lord . . . , not turning aside to the right or to the left."

When he was 16, "while he was still young," he gave his heart to God; when he was 20, he began to clean things up in the city in a big way. The altars of Baal were broken down "under his direction." He went personally to see that the idols were destroyed. As for the incense altars and places where people worshiped Asherah, he cut them down himself. He burned all the wooden idols, scattering the ashes on the graves of those who had sacrificed to them. The metal images were ground to dust, just as Moses had destroyed

170

the golden calf in the wilderness.

Having cleaned out all the idols from Jerusalem, Josiah went throughout Israel and did the same in every city and village. Since the Assyrians had gone back to their homeland by now, there was nobody to stop him.

As he traveled through the country, he asked for offerings to help repair the Temple, which had been badly damaged during the reign of Manasseh and his wicked son, Amon. Poor as the people were, they gave what they could. Josiah used this money to buy stone and lumber and to pay the workmen.

At this time a wonderful discovery was made. As the money for the repair of the Temple was being taken out of the room where it had been stored, Hilkiah the high priest noticed a roll of parchment. Picking it up, he saw that it was "the Book of the Law of the Lord that had been given through Moses." Somebody had hidden it long ago to keep it safe from enemies.

Excitedly Hilkiah called to Shaphan the scribe, "I have

found the Book of the Law in the temple of the Lord."

Shaphan could hardly believe his ears. This was too good to be true. Everybody thought the books of Moses had been destroyed long ago. Running to Hilkiah, he eagerly took the book from the high priest's trembling hands.

Yes! It *was* the long-lost Temple copy of the sacred book written by Israel's greatest leader. With the book clutched in his hands, Shaphan hurried to tell Josiah the wonderful news. Then he read long passages from it to him.

As Josiah listened he was deeply troubled. Suddenly he realized how far the children of Israel had fallen into sin and how deeply they must have disappointed God.

You see, people did not have Bibles in their homes in those days. Knowledge of God's will depended largely on people's memories, and they weren't too good. That's why the discovery of this book was so very, very important.

You can imagine what Josiah thought as he heard the Ten Commandments read to him from the sacred scrolls for the first time in his life:

"You shall have no other gods before me.

"You shall not make for yourself an idol. . . .

"You shall not misuse the name of the Lord your God. . . .

"Remember the Sabbath day by keeping it holy. . . .

"Honor your father and your mother. . . .

"You shall not murder.

"You shall not commit adultery.

173

← PAINTING BY MANNING DE V. LEE

When Shaphan the scribe read to King Josiah the counsels of God from the sacred scroll that had been lost so many years in the rubble of the Temple, the king was moved with grief.

"You shall not steal.

"You shall not give false testimony. . . .

"You shall not covet." [1]

"We have broken them all!" the young king must have cried, as he thought of all the wicked things his people had been doing.

Then in silent awe he listened as Shaphan read, "However, if you do not obey the Lord your God and do not carefully follow all his commands and decrees I am giving you today, all these curses will come upon you and overtake you: . . .

"You will be cursed when you come in and cursed when you go out.

"The Lord will send on you curses, confusion and rebuke." [2]

The king was shaken with dismay and grief. "Go and inquire of the Lord for me . . . ," he said to his officials. "Great is the Lord's anger that is poured out on us because our fathers have not kept the word of the Lord; they have not acted in accordance with all that is written in this book."

Hilkiah and Shaphan went to Huldah the prophetess for advice. She told them that Judah would indeed be punished for all the evil it had done, but this punishment would not come in the days of Josiah because he had humbled himself before God and wept for the transgressions of his people.

When Josiah received this message, he called everybody in

174

Jerusalem and Judah to meet him in the Temple. When they arrived, "He read in their hearing all the words of the Book of the Covenant, which had been found in the temple of the Lord."

Publicly he made his own promise to the Lord to "keep his commands, regulations and decrees with all his heart and all his soul." Then he asked everyone who would join him in this rededication to God to stand.

While the people were repentant, he told them of his plan to keep the Passover again. They were glad. "The Passover had not been observed like this in Israel since the days of the prophet Samuel." But that was the last Passover old Jerusalem and Solomon's Temple ever saw.

When good king Josiah died, Judah's last hope died with him. Little more than 20 years later, both the city and the Temple were in ruins.

[1] Exodus 20:1-17.
[2] Deuteronomy 28:15-20.

The Call of Jeremiah

(Jeremiah 1)

MONG those who wept at the death of King Josiah was "Jeremiah son of Hilkiah," perhaps the same Hilkiah who found the book of the law in the Temple treasure chest.

Jeremiah and Josiah must have been about the same age, because Josiah was 21 when God called Jeremiah to be a prophet. These two young men grew up together with the same hopes and ideals. They worked together trying to remove all idol worship and bring the people back to God. No wonder Jeremiah cried when his good friend died.

As a boy, Jeremiah never dreamed he would be a prophet when he grew up. He didn't want to be one. He loved the Lord and hoped to serve Him as a faithful priest like his father. But to be a prophet like Elijah, Elisha, or Isaiah, oh, no! He wasn't thinking of a job like that.

But God had His eye on this boy. He saw that Jeremiah was faithful in his work. He was a boy who could be trusted. One day God spoke to him and said something very surprising. "Before I

◄— PAINTING BY RUSSELL HARLAN

Called by God to be a prophet, Jeremiah made the plea that he did not know how to speak, but God touched his lips and said, "Behold, I have put my words in thy mouth."

formed you in the womb I knew you, before you were born I set you apart; I appointed you as a prophet to the nations."

Jeremiah found this hard to believe, and begged to be excused, just like Moses when God called him at the burning bush. "Ah, Sovereign Lord," Jeremiah said. "I do not know how to speak; I am only a child." But God put His hand on Jeremiah's mouth and said, "Now, I have put my words in your mouth."

This was an even more wonderful experience than Isaiah's calling, because though Isaiah's lips were touched by a live coal from the altar, Jeremiah's lips were touched by the finger of God.

Then God said to this rather bashful young man, "See, today I appoint you over nations and kingdoms to uproot and tear down, to destroy and overthrow, to build and to plant."

Jeremiah didn't feel like pulling down or destroying anything. He would rather have a more peaceful life. And he didn't like talking to people; crowds frightened him.

God understood. Patiently He said, "Do not be terrified by them." There was no need for fear. "Today," said the Lord, "I have made you a fortified city, an iron pillar and a bronze wall to stand against the whole land—against the kings of Judah, its officials, its priests and the people of the land. They will fight against you but will not overcome you, for I am with you and will rescue you."

Wonderful promise! What more could God offer to do for this young man He wanted in His service? God promised He would take away all Jeremiah's fear, all his feelings of weakness,

178

and make his sagging backbone like an iron pillar. He would make him like a city with bronze walls, which no enemy could break down. And through the darkest days God would be with him to deliver him.

Jeremiah accepted his call and became one of the greatest prophets of all time.

Perhaps someday God will call you to work for Him. If He does, remember His promises to Jeremiah. Let His fingers touch your lips. Let His words be your words. And don't be afraid of people. "Do not be terrified by them," for God will be with you always, to deliver you.

Judah's Last Chance

(2 Chronicles 36:1-5; Jeremiah 3:22-11:22)

TIME was running out for Judah and Jerusalem, but the people did not realize it, and they didn't care. After Josiah's death, everything went wrong. His sons were not a bit like him. They brought back idol worship again, and then they had one trouble after another.

Hardly had Jehoahaz become king when Pharaoh Necho deposed him and put his brother Jehoiakim on the throne. At the same time Pharaoh demanded payment of 75 pounds (34 kilograms) of silver and three fourths of a pound (0.3 kilogram) of gold.

By taxing the people heavily, Jehoiakim raised the money, but he had just paid off the Egyptians when the Babylonians arrived. They looted the Temple and took a number of young men from the royal family captive, including Daniel and his friends.

During these dark and terrible days, Jeremiah tried to bring to king and people God's last call to repentance. The depth of love in his messages is something to wonder at.

180

"Return, faithless people," he earnestly pleaded in the name of God. "I will cure you of backsliding."

" 'If you will return, O Israel, return to me,' declares the Lord. 'If you put your detestable idols out of my sight and no longer go astray, and if in a truthful, just and righteous way you swear, "As surely as the Lord lives," then the nations will be blessed by him and in him they will glory.' "

The people still had a chance to avoid being carried away captive. They had only to repent. "O Jerusalem," cried the prophet, "wash the evil from your heart and be saved."

If just one honest man could be found in the city, God said, all would be forgiven. "Go up and down the streets of Jerusalem, look around and consider, search through her squares. If you can find but one person who deals honestly and seeks the truth, I will forgive this city."

"Reform your ways and your actions," God pleaded

through Jeremiah, "and I will let you live in this place . . . for ever and ever."

How tenderly God spoke to these people who had turned their backs on Him and disobeyed Him so many times! How much He must have loved them to have offered them full pardon after they had been so wicked!

Did they listen? Did they care? Did they repent? No, indeed.

When God said to them, "Stand at the crossroads and look; ask for the ancient paths, ask where the good way is, and walk in it, and you will find rest for your souls," they answered, "We will not walk in it."

The people had been evil for so long that they had come to like wrong better than right. "My people love it this way," lamented the prophet. They didn't *want* to be good anymore.

When the priests, rulers, and wealthy merchants laughed at him because of his simple, old-fashioned teachings, Jeremiah said to them, "This is what the Lord says: 'Let not the wise man boast of his wisdom or the strong man boast of his strength or the rich man boast of his riches, but let him who boasts boast about this: that he understands and knows me, that I am the Lord, who exercises kindness, justice and righteousness on earth, for in these I delight,' declares the Lord."

As the days and months went by and nobody took any notice of him, Jeremiah's warnings became stronger and stronger.

"Listen to what the Lord says," he cried. "O house of Israel, . . . I am bringing a distant nation against you—an

182

ancient and enduring nation, a people whose language you do not know. . . .

"They will devour your harvests and food, . . . your flocks and herds, . . . your vines and fig trees. . . .

"As you have forsaken me and served foreign gods in your own land, so now you will serve foreigners in a land not your own."

Again, he said, "I will bring on them a disaster they cannot escape." "I will punish them. Their young men will die by the sword, their sons and daughters by famine."

But nobody paid any attention to his warnings. They called him a prophet of doom and said he didn't know what he was talking about. Had not Jerusalem stood for hundreds of years? Would it not stand for hundreds more?

Sorrowfully Jeremiah answered them, "Even the stork in the sky knows her appointed seasons, and the dove, the swift and the thrush observe the time of their migration. But my people do not know the requirements of the Lord."

Storks, doves, swifts, thrushes—and many other birds— all know their time to migrate, and obey it. But God's people, blinded by sin, couldn't see that the hour of His judgment had come.

Escape From a Dungeon

(*Jeremiah 20:1-9; 26:20-23; 36:1-23; 37:12-38:13*)

AS JEREMIAH continued to warn the people of coming judgment, he got into trouble with Judah's leaders. After one sermon in which he had said that Jerusalem would become "desolate and deserted" if it did not return to God, he was arrested and brought before the officials of the city.

"This man should be sentenced to death," said his accusers, "because he has prophesied against this city. You have heard it with your own ears!"

The priests and officials were so angry they would have killed him then and there if a few strong friends had not spoken up for him. As it was, another prophet, Uriah, who had given exactly the same message, was put to death.

After another of Jeremiah's sermons, Pashhur, the high priest and chief officer in the Temple, beat him. Then he put Jeremiah in the stocks and left him there all night. When Jeremiah was set free the next morning, he told Pashhur what was going to happen to him.

"This is what the Lord says: . . . 'I will hand all Judah over to the king of Babylon, who will carry them away to Babylon or put them to the sword. . . . And you, Pashhur, and all who live in your house will go into exile to Babylon. There you will die and be buried, you and all your friends to whom you have prophesied lies.' "

So many people opposed him or laughed at him, that it was hard for Jeremiah to keep on with his work. "I am ridiculed all day long," he murmured. "Everyone mocks me." More than once he thought of giving up. "I will not mention him or speak any more in his name," he said. But he couldn't do it. The word of God was like a burning fire in his bones, and he couldn't keep quiet.

Thinking that if he wrote out all the messages God had given him, the people might take more notice, he dictated them to Baruch, who wrote them on a scroll. Then he had Baruch go and read the scroll in the Temple. Some of the

officials became interested, and asked Baruch to read it privately to them. But when King Jehoiakim heard about the scroll, he sent for it. Whenever three or four columns had been read to him, "the king cut them off with a scribe's knife and threw them into the firepot."

After Zedekiah came to the throne, Jeremiah was accused of treason. He was caught leaving the city to go to the land of Benjamin, and the guard thought he was going to join the Babylonians.

"That's not true!" said Jeremiah. But they wouldn't listen to him. He was beaten and put in prison.

When King Zedekiah heard what had happened, he sent for Jeremiah and asked him if there was any new word from God. Yes, said the prophet, there was. "You will be handed over to the king of Babylon."

For this he was sent back to prison. But even so he kept on preaching his message: " 'This city will certainly be handed

186

over to the army of the king of Babylon, who will capture it.' "

Finally the officials could stand it no longer. They went to Zedekiah and said, " 'This man should be put to death. He is discouraging the soldiers who are left in this city, . . . by the things he is saying to them.' "

Zedekiah said they could do what they liked with him. So they "put him into the cistern . . . , which was in the courtyard of the guard." It must have been very deep, for they needed ropes to let him down. At the bottom it was wet and muddy, and "Jeremiah sank down in the mud."

It was a terrible place for anybody to be imprisoned, let alone a man as old as Jeremiah must have been by now. How cold it was! How tiring, with no place to sit or lie down! How uncomfortable, with his feet squishing in the mud all the time! Every minute must have seemed an hour and every hour an eternity.

Only one person in all Jerusalem cared, and that was Ebed-Melech. He was not an Israelite but "a Cushite, an official in

the royal palace." He liked the old prophet and knew what a good man he was.

Bravely going to the king, he told him what a wrong thing had been done to Jeremiah. "They have thrown him into a cistern, where he will starve to death," he said. Then he asked permission to take the old man out of that awful pit.

Zedekiah agreed, and told Ebed-Melech to take 30 men to help him.

How glad Jeremiah must have been to see the kind face of that dear Black man looking down from the top of the dungeon! I can almost hear him saying, "God bless you, son, for coming to my rescue."

Ebed-Melech sent down ropes. As Jeremiah reached for it, he found a bundle of rags tied to it.

"Put these old rags and worn-out clothes under your arms to pad the ropes," called Ebed-Melech, "so the ropes won't hurt you." How very thoughtful of him!

Jeremiah did, and the men began to pull. At last he reached the top, muddy, starving, and shivering with cold, but, oh, so glad to be out in the sunlight again!

We are not told what happened to Ebed-Melech, but I am sure God must have blessed him for his kindness. As for Jeremiah, he stayed in the courtyard of the guard "until the day that Jerusalem was captured."

← PAINTING BY HERBERT RUDEEN

Jeremiah blessed the kind Ethiopian who pulled him up out of the muddy dungeon where Zedekiah had thrown him for daring to tell him he would be overcome by Babylon.

Jerusalem Captured

(2 Kings 24:8-25:21; 2 Chronicles 36:8-21)

EVERYTHING Jeremiah prophesied about Jerusalem came true. Just as he had said, the Babylonians took the city and destroyed it.

They came first, you remember, in the days of Jehoiakim and took away Daniel and his friends and some of the treasures in the Temple. After Jehoiakim's death, they came again during the three-month reign of his son Jehoiachin.

This time they took the young king, his mother, his attendants, his nobles, 7,000 soldiers, and all the skilled craftsmen in the city, to Babylon. They also took "all the treasures from the temple of the Lord and from the royal palace"—just as Isaiah told Hezekiah would happen someday.

In place of Jehoiakim, Nebuchadnezzar, king of Babylon, put Jehoiachin's uncle Zedekiah on the throne, thinking he would be loyal to him. But he wasn't. After a few years he rebelled, and Nebuchadnezzar's armies came back in great fury.

190

JERUSALEM CAPTURED

This time the siege of Jerusalem lasted two and a half years. As it went on, all the food in the city was eaten. "The famine in the city had become so severe that there was no food for the people to eat."

At last the Babylonians broke through the walls. Seeing there was no hope of holding out any longer, "the whole army fled at night," the king with them. They got as far as Jericho, but the Babylonians caught up with them.

Zedekiah was taken before Nebuchadnezzar, who ordered that his sons be killed before his eyes. Then they blinded him, "bound him with bronze shackles and took him to Babylon."

That was the miserable fate of the last of the kings of Judah. Little more than 400 years had passed since David's coronation, with all the high hopes he had that day. Now his throne was gone, and as far as anyone could see at the moment, his line had died out.

As for Jerusalem, Nebuchadnezzar sent his commander of the imperial guard to do a thorough job of destruction. "He set fire to the temple of the Lord, the royal palace and all the houses of Jerusalem. Every important building he burned down." Then his soldiers went to work on the walls until they had broken them down completely.

Nothing was left of Solomon's beautiful Temple. The

two large bronze pillars and "the movable stands and the bronze Sea" were broken into pieces and all the metal was carried off to Babylon. Nobody was left in or near the city except a few very poor people. The rest were taken away. "So Judah went into captivity, away from her land."

How sad, how very, very sad! The angels must have wept as they thought of all that God had done for the children of Israel since He brought them out of Egypt. He had given them the mighty miracles at the Red Sea and the Jordan, the glorious victories of Joshua, the wisdom and fame of Solomon.

But now all God's wonderful plans for Israel had ended in failure! What a disappointment! What heartbreak!

And what about the promises to Abraham, Isaac, and Jacob? What about the promise to Adam and Eve in the Garden of Eden? Was God's beautiful plan wrecked forever? Had He lost the battle with evil?

No. Dark though the night had become, a star of hope still glimmered. Faint though it was, it would grow brighter and brighter with the passing years.

God is never defeated. Far across the desert, in old Babylon, He had already started to build again.